BLUEPRINT
Assemblies

Jim Fitzsimmons

Rhona Whiteford

Stanley Thornes (Publishers) Ltd

First published in 1989 by:
Stanley Thornes (Publishers) Ltd
Old Station Drive
Leckhampton
CHELTENHAM GL53 0DN
England

Reprinted 1990

British Library Cataloguing in Publication Data
Fitzsimmons, Jim
  Assemblies. – (Blueprints).
  1. Schools. Morning assembly. Activities
  I. Title   II. Whiteford, Rhona   III. Series
  377'.1
  ISBN 0–7487–0089–7

Typeset by Kalligraphics Ltd, Horley, Surrey.
Printed in Great Britain at The Bath Press, Avon.

CONTENTS

INTRODUCTION

Blueprints: Assemblies provides 15 complete, ready-made, photocopiable scripts for class assemblies. They contain speaking parts for children, poems, prayers, suggestions for music and short plays which can be performed as part of the assembly. In addition there are ideas for props, backdrops and staging, checklists of items required, and cross-curricular flowcharts to show how the assemblies can be integrated into topics and other class work.

The assemblies are intended for flexible use: they can be performed complete or can be adapted or cut to meet your own needs with the minimum of effort. The assemblies are at three levels of difficulty: the first aimed broadly at reception-age children, the second at middle infants and the third at top infants and lower juniors. They vary in length, depending on topic and age group. The longest take about 20 minutes (depending on delivery), but all can be cut by omitting the play or other sections to make 10-minute assemblies if required. You will find that the assemblies are cross-curricular and multi-cultural: they cover topics of moral and social importance to children (and adults) whatever their racial or religious backgrounds.

Planning the assembly

1. If you are using the assembly as part of some topic work, your preparation will start a few weeks before the performance. Use the topic web at the front of each script to help with your planning. Any items which are to be written by the children can be done as part of their classwork, as can paintings for illustration. These paintings are best mounted on brightly coloured activity paper and should be as large as possible so that they can be seen at the back of the hall. Help the children with the scale of their paintings.

2. Collect all the special props and resources in advance. These can often be loaned by children in your class, by other classes or by staff or friends of the school. Some LEAs have a museum or library loans service for artefacts and paintings. A checklist of all the props and items you will need is included with each assembly, as instant reference for you.

3. A special backdrop for an assembly is going to take a lot of time and effort, so it might be a good idea to leave a spot in the hall for a display board for assembly topics. This can be changed every time a different class does an assembly, and it will provide a varied interest point for visitors and children alike. As the whole school will have joined in the assembly, the display will have a greater significance for them than some of the other displays they see.

4. If you do decide to create special backdrops, those

we have suggested can become the base of a classroom display of the work the children have done towards the assembly, but plan this well in advance. All the assemblies will work perfectly well without the backdrops or the illustrations suggested, but for the youngest children (and indeed adults) something to look at often helps to keep attention.

Preparing the scripts

1. Duplicate one whole script for yourself as a master copy, and blank out any sections you don't want with paper, before duplication for the children.

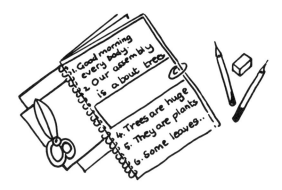

2. Duplicate another copy which you can then cut up into individual parts and paste on card for each child.

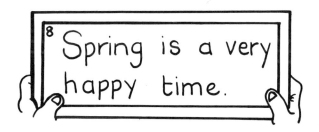

3. For the plays, duplicate the whole play for each actor so that he or she can see the continuity.

4. Have a spare set of children's parts so that, if any child is away on the day, you can give these out to the good readers or read them yourself.

Practising the assembly

1. Start practising well before the event so that children have a chance to memorise their words if they are not capable of reading well enough. Let the children hold their scripts even if they cannot read them, because, as they practise their lines and eventually learn to say them, they may begin to recognise each word.

2. Go through the spoken parts in the classroom first of all, as you can do this in any spare 10 minutes when the hall is unavailable. From the start, arrange the children in speaking order so they get used to the sequence and remember the lines that come before their own. Remember that some children may have more than one part and will need to be organised for their second set of cues.

3. Practise the assembly as often as possible, making sure the children project their voices and face the audience, and that they don't fall into the trap of covering their faces with their reading. If children are going to hold up illustrations, practise this too, with large sheets of paper. This will allow them to get used to the manoeuvres involved: holding at the correct height, picking up and putting down, not rustling, etc.

4. Do plan the children's positions in the hall as early as possible and check how many stage blocks, benches, chairs and display boards you will need. Also check the availability of these large items for the day you want them, as they may be shared by other classes.

5. Practise the playlets in costume as soon as possible to get over any practical problems of movement in costume, or design of costume, e.g. hats being insecure.

6. Where scenery or props changes are needed, make sure these are well rehearsed, that props are close at hand and that there is a minimum of steps or stage blocks to negotiate.

7. When there are two scenes needed in a play or assembly, mount them on each side of a length of corrugated card two metres deep. Have two children as stage hands to move props and set the scene and then hold the sheet up during the performance. When the time comes to change the scene, cross over as shown.

8. Arrange seats and props in place the night before the assembly, if possible.

9. Allow children to carry smaller illustrations in with them so that they won't be trodden on. Get the children to lay them face down on the floor in front of them, ready for use. After speaking, they should put their pictures face down on the floor once more.

10. Decide whether the children are to be ready seated when the audience enters or whether you will teach them to walk in, in the right order, and sit down quietly as the audience waits and the rest of the school gather in their places.

COLOUR

BACKDROP

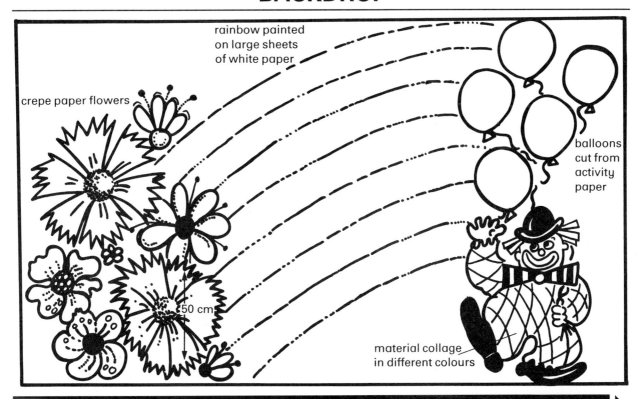

rainbow painted on large sheets of white paper

crepe paper flowers

balloons cut from activity paper

50 cm

material collage in different colours

CHECKLIST

- Backdrop

- Children's seating arrangements

- Card binoculars, telescope, glasses

- Eight paintings for the poem 'A Rainbow of Faces'

- Poster of children of different races

- Child's swimwear, towel, sunglasses and suntan lotion

- Three easels or boards to hold the camouflage pictures

- Three camouflage scenes – snow, golden corn (wheat), green leaves

- Three camouflaged animals – polar bear, harvest mouse, grass-snake

- The word 'camouflage' written on card

- The word 'danger' written on card

- Painting of toadstool

- Painting of snake

- Painting or model of traffic-lights showing 'stop', i.e. with red brightest

- Child's red outfit

- Child's green outfit

- Four to six paintings of children's favourite colours

- 'Strange colours' painting of bananas and peas

- 'Strange colours' painting of bread and chips

- Four large lollies (green, red, yellow, purple)

- Tie-dye exhibits (display and pieces of material)

- Poster of blind person and guide dog

3

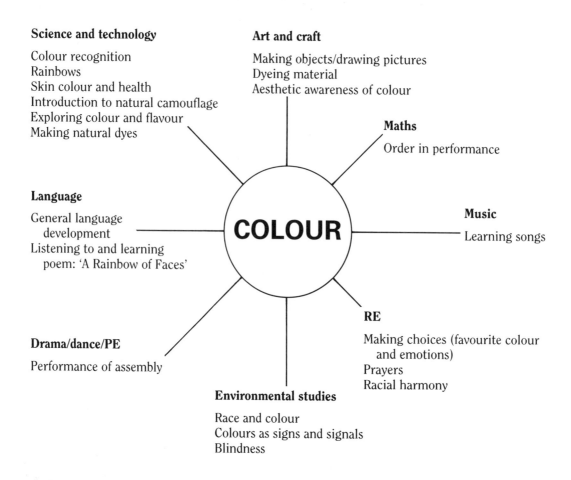

Science and technology

Colour recognition
Rainbows
Skin colour and health
Introduction to natural camouflage
Exploring colour and flavour
Making natural dyes

Art and craft

Making objects/drawing pictures
Dyeing material
Aesthetic awareness of colour

Maths

Order in performance

Language

General language
  development
Listening to and learning
  poem: 'A Rainbow of Faces'

COLOUR

Music

Learning songs

RE

Making choices (favourite colour
  and emotions)
Prayers
Racial harmony

Drama/dance/PE

Performance of assembly

Environmental studies

Race and colour
Colours as signs and signals
Blindness

THE ASSEMBLY: Colour

1. Good morning.

2. Our assembly is all about colour.

3. The world is full of beautiful colours and we've been using our eyes to look about us.

The first three children pick up binoculars (two cardboard tubes), telescope (one cardboard tube) and a large pair of cardboard glasses. They look about the hall, peering at the ceiling, into corners, at children, teachers and parents.

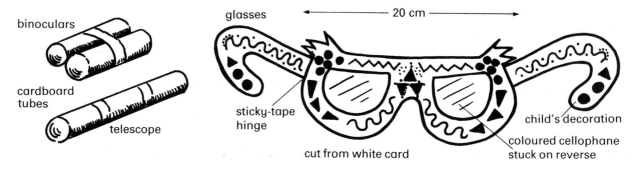

binoculars

cardboard tubes

telescope

glasses

20 cm

sticky-tape hinge

cut from white card

child's decoration

coloured cellophane stuck on reverse

4. We have learnt a poem about colours.

If children can't manage to memorise the whole poem, use one child for each couplet. Let the child or children who read the couplet about a colour do the illustration for it. Choose one or two items for each colour and draw big, bold pictures which the children can colour. Children who are capable can draw their own objects. Mount the paintings on the appropriate colour of activity paper. Here are some suggestions of what you might draw.

POEM

A Rainbow of Faces

5. Red is so happy it makes me quite hot,
With red I'm excited, I bubble and pop.

6. Blue is so chilly I think of ice,
It's sky and water and rather nice.

5

7. Yellow's for custard and sunshine bright,
   And stars in heaven which shine at night.

8. Green is the colour of grass in the spring,
   Of cucumbers cool and an emerald ring.

9. This colour is dark as the deepest hole,
   Black as a cat, the colour of coal.

10. White is the colour of clothes for a baby,
    Twinkling bright, as fresh as a daisy.

11. Children are black, white and brownish too,
    Look at the one who sits next to you.

12. The whole world is made of a rainbow of faces,
    The people of all different countries and races.

13. Lots of different people live in Britain
    and they have different coloured skins.

    Child holds up poster of children of different races. *Child Education* is a good
    source of such posters. Alternatively, if you have children of different ethnic groups
    in the class, ask if two or three of them are willing to stand up, smiling, at this
    point.

14. Dark skins are protected from sunburn.

15. People with white skins like to get a nice suntan.

    Child wearing swimsuit, carrying towel and suntan lotion.

16. Animals use colours to keep safe from other animals
    which eat them.

17. They also use colours to hide from animals
    they want to eat.

18. Can you see this polar bear against the white snow?

    Child holds bear against the polar snow scene on the easel or board.

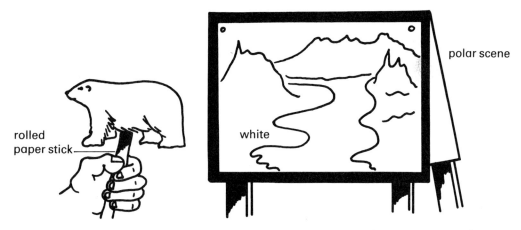

19. Polar bears eat sea-lions and the sea-lions can't see the bear sneaking up on them.

20. Can you see this mouse in the golden corn?

Child holds harvest mouse against the scene on the easel or board.

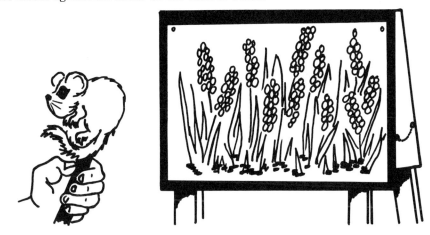

21. His colour helps him to hide from birds.

22. Can you see this grass-snake in the green leaves?

Child holds snake against the picture of green grass and leaves.

23. His colour makes him hard to see.

7

24. The way animals use colour is called camouflage.

Child holds up a large card with the word 'camouflage' written on it.

25. Animals and plants use bright colours and patterns to warn of danger.

Child holds up large card with the word 'danger' written on it.

26. This toadstool says: "I'm poisonous. Don't eat me."

Child holds up painting of toadstool.

red and white

27. This snake says: "I'm poisonous. Don't touch me."

Child holds up painting of snake.

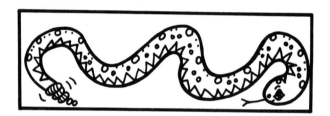

28. We use the colour red to warn people of danger.

29. Red for the traffic-light that says, "Stop!"

Child holds up painting/model of traffic-lights.

bright red

30. Red for the man on the pelican crossing who says, "Don't cross!"

Child wears a red shirt and trousers or a red leotard and tights, and stands still and straight like the figure on the traffic-light signal.

31. The man on the pelican crossing who says it is safe to cross wears green like me.

Child wears green and stands in a walking position like the traffic-signal.

32. We all like different colours. Sing this song with us and think about your favourite colour.

SONG

'Sing a Rainbow' from *Apusskidu*, published by A. & C. Black, is sung by the whole school.

33. We've painted some things in our favourite colours.

Choose four to six children to hold up their own paintings, again mounted on card of the same colour as the subject, and to say a short sentence such as, 'I painted chocolate ice-cream', 'I painted oranges', or 'I painted a red bus'.

34. Wouldn't it be strange if things weren't the colours we expected?

35. Wouldn't it be strange if bananas were pink and peas were blue?

Child holds up painting of same.

36. Wouldn't it be funny if bread was purple and chips were red?

Child holds up painting of same.

37. It's a good job they aren't because the colour usually tells us what flavour the food is.

38. Lime-flavoured things are usually green, because limes are green.

Child holds up picture of green lolly.

39. Strawberry-flavoured things are red because strawberries are red.

Child holds up red lolly.

40. Lemon-flavoured things are yellow because lemons are yellow.

Child holds up yellow lolly.

41. Blackcurrant-flavoured things are purple because blackcurrants are purple.

Child holds up purple lolly.

40 cm   yellow   green   red   purple

42. Some foods have strong colours and we dyed some material with foods.

Child points to a display of tie-dyed materials.

43. We used onions to dye this material brown.

Child holds up example or goes to display and points to it.

44. We used blackberries to dye this material blue.

Child holds up example.

45. We used saffron to dye this material yellow.

Child holds up example.

46. When it has been raining we sometimes see a rainbow like this.

Child points to rainbow on backdrop.

47. The colours of the rainbow are . . .

Whole class or group speaks together:
'Red, orange, yellow, green, blue, indigo, violet'.

48. Blind people can't see the wonderful colours,
but they can feel and hear and smell
better than people who can see.

Child holds up poster of person with guide dog.

PRAYER
---

49. Hands together, eyes closed.

This prayer can be read by the teacher or by a child who is a good reader (or who has a good memory!).

Thank you God for the rainbow of colours
we see every day, and for the flowers,
animals and people of different colours
who make up this beautiful world.   Amen

50. Will you sing this song with us to finish our assembly?

SONG

Choose from 'The Ink is Black, the Page is White', 'I have seen the Golden Sunshine' and 'Stand Up, Clap Hands, Shout "Thank you, Lord"', all from *Someone's Singing, Lord*, published by A. & C. Black; 'Every Colour Under the Sun' from the book of the same name, published by Ward Lock Educational.

BACKDROP

CHECKLIST

- Backdrop
- Children's seating arrangements
- Record-player
- Record: 'My Grandfather's Clock' sung by Val Doonican
- Painting – day and night
- Painting – getting up
- Painting – having lunch
- Painting – playing
- Painting – watching TV
- Painting – sleeping
- Calendar
- Birthdays graph
- Winter picture
- Spring picture
- Summer picture
- Autumn picture
- Clock face
- Picture of digital clock
- Picture of sundial
- Egg-timer or picture of one
- Picture of cuckoo-clock
- Stop-watch
- Kitchen timer
- Watch
- Travel clock
- Picture of migrating swallows
- Picture of squirrel
- Small cross-section of tree-trunk

TOPIC WEB

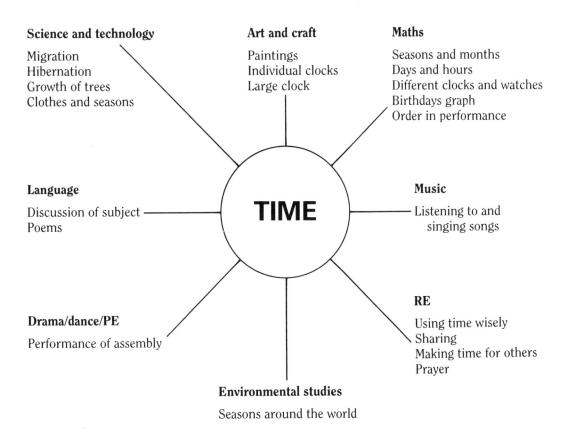

Science and technology

Migration
Hibernation
Growth of trees
Clothes and seasons

Art and craft

Paintings
Individual clocks
Large clock

Maths

Seasons and months
Days and hours
Different clocks and watches
Birthdays graph
Order in performance

Language

Discussion of subject
Poems

TIME

Music

Listening to and
singing songs

Drama/dance/PE

Performance of assembly

RE

Using time wisely
Sharing
Making time for others
Prayer

Environmental studies

Seasons around the world

13

MUSIC

For entry into the assembly play 'My Grandfather's Clock' or the nursery rhyme 'Hickory Dickory Dock'.

1. Good morning everybody. Welcome to our assembly. It is all about time.

SONG

A hymn or song can be sung at this stage, perhaps 'Morning has Broken' from *Someone's Singing, Lord*, published by A. & C. Black.

2. Time never stops. When the sky is light it is called day. When it is dark it is called night.

Child holds up picture.

3. The sun comes up in the morning. I get out of bed and have my breakfast.

Child holds up picture.

4. At nine o'clock I go to school and we work in our classroom until twelve o'clock. Then I have my lunch.

Child holds up picture.

5. At half past three I go home and play outside.

Child holds up picture.

6. At five o'clock I have my tea,
   and then I watch television.

   Child holds up picture.

7. At seven o'clock I get ready for bed and
   I sleep through the night until the next day.

   Child holds up picture.

POEM

The man in the moon
Looked out of the moon
And this is what he said,
Now that I'm getting up it's time
All children were in bed.

SONG

Twinkle twinkle little star,
How I wonder what you are.
Up above the world so high,
Like a diamond in the sky.
Twinkle twinkle little star,
How I wonder what you are.

8. There are seven days in one week.

   The whole class says the names: 'Sunday, Monday, Tuesday, Wednesday, Thursday,
   Friday, Saturday'.

SONG

This can be sung by a small group or by the whole class.

Monday's child is fair of face.
Tuesday's child is full of grace.
Wednesday's child is full of woe.
Thursday's child has far to go.
Friday's child is loving and giving.
Saturday's child works hard for its living.
But the child that is born on the Sabbath day
Is bonny and blithe and good and gay.

9. The days make weeks and there are four weeks in one month.

10. We use calendars to help us know what day or month it is.

   Child holds up calendar.

11. There are twelve months in one year.

   Whole class or group chant: 'January, February, March, April, May, June, July, August, September, October, November, December'.

12. We have our birthdays in these months and we have made a graph to show when our birthdays are.

   To show in which month his or her birthday falls, each child writes his or her name on a cake and sticks it on the chart. The chart should be prepared prior to the assembly.

13. The world moves round the sun and it takes one year to go all the way round.

14. Because of this, things change in many parts of the world. These changes are called seasons.

15. Winter is the first season. It is very cold and we have to wear warm clothes.

Child dressed in gloves, woolly hat, scarf, overcoat and boots holds up a winter picture.

16. Spring is next. Things start to grow again and the days get longer.

Child dressed in raincoat and wellies holds up a spring picture.

17. In the summer the days are long and hot. We can go out for day trips and picnics. Sometimes we can go to the seaside.

Child dressed in bathing-costume and sunglasses holds up a summer picture.

18. In the autumn fruits ripen and leaves change colour. Some animals get ready to hibernate. The days begin to get shorter.

Child dressed in jeans, anorak and wellies holds up an autumn picture.

19. We cannot see time but we can measure it.

20. We can use lots of things to measure time.
    We can use clocks.

21. Some clocks have fingers or hands which point to
    the time.

Child holds up clock face.

1 m or
50 cm
diameter

22. Some clocks show the time with numbers.
    This is called a digital clock.

Child holds up a picture.

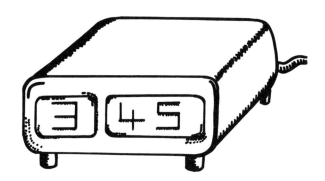

23. This is a sundial. The shadows on the sundial
    show the time. Sundials must be outside so that
    the sun can shine on them. If it is a cloudy day,
    there will be no shadows so you will not be able
    to tell the time.

Child holds up a picture.

24. This is an egg-timer.
We watch the sand trickle down through the hole.
When all the sand is at the bottom, the egg is cooked.

Child holds up a picture.

25. This is a cuckoo-clock.
The cuckoo comes out every hour to say, "Cuckoo".

Child holds up cut-out picture.

26. This is a stop-watch. It tells us how much time
we take to run a race.

Child holds up a stop-watch.

27. This is a kitchen timer. It tells us when it is time
to take a cake out of the oven.

Child holds up a kitchen timer.

28. A watch is a clock we can wear.

Child shows the watch he or she is wearing.

29. A travel clock is one we can take on holiday.

Child holds up a travel clock.

30. We see clocks everywhere: in town, on churches, in the park.

SONG

A song can be sung at this stage, by the class or by the whole school. You could sing 'At Half Past Three We Go Home to Tea', from *Someone's Singing, Lord*, published by A. & C. Black.

31. People need clocks and calendars, but animals do not.

32. Swallows know when to meet to fly south for the winter.

Child holds up a picture of gathering swallows.

33. Squirrels know when to gather extra food to last them through the winter.

Child holds up picture.

34. We can tell how old a tree is by counting the rings inside the trunk.
There is one ring for each year of its life.

If possible, child holds up small cross-section of tree-trunk.

POEM

This poem can be read by one child or by several children each reading one verse.

Time

Time is always passing
    It never stops or stays.
It can be hours or minutes
    Or weeks or months or days.

Sometimes it goes slowly
    And then it's just no fun.
Sometimes it goes by so fast
    We wonder where it's gone.

There's never any time to waste
    But may be time to spare,
Whenever someone's feeling sad
    We should take time to care.

Just try your best in everything
    And very soon you'll find
There's nothing that you cannot do,
    All it takes is time.

BACKDROP

A huge card is positioned on the stage and the children are grouped on either side of it. Try to invite parents – especially mums – to the assembly.

CHECKLIST

- Backdrop

- Children's seating arrangements

- Children's writing, 'I love Mum because . . .'

- Items or clothing connected with jobs many mums do at home: cleaning, washing, cooking, ironing, looking after baby

- Painting and writing about mums who have an outside job

- Painting of Simnel cake

- Play: *The Legend of Simon and Nell*
  backdrop
  props: table, bowls, spatulas, ingredients (empty packets of flour, raisins, marzipan)

- Presents for the children to take to their mothers

- Chairs for parents

Make sure that you deal sensitively with children from non-standard family groups.

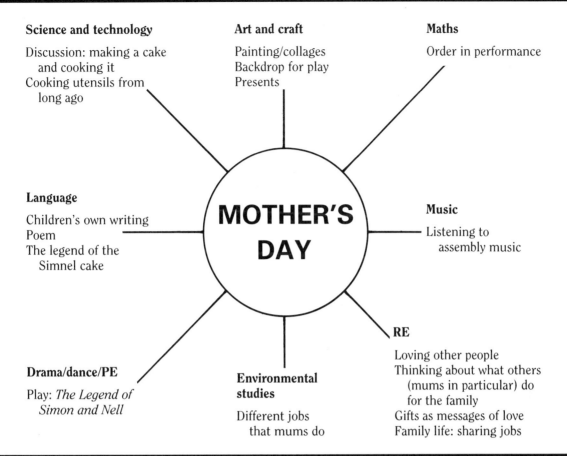

Science and technology

Discussion: making a cake
and cooking it
Cooking utensils from
long ago

Art and craft

Painting/collages
Backdrop for play
Presents

Maths

Order in performance

Language

Children's own writing
Poem
The legend of the
Simnel cake

MOTHER'S DAY

Music

Listening to
assembly music

Drama/dance/PE

Play: *The Legend of
Simon and Nell*

**Environmental
studies**

Different jobs
that mums do

RE

Loving other people
Thinking about what others
(mums in particular) do
for the family
Gifts as messages of love
Family life: sharing jobs

THE ASSEMBLY: Mother's Day ▶

1. Good morning everybody and welcome to
our Mother's Day assembly.

2. We have been thinking about our mothers
and why we love them.

Here a selection of children can read what they have written about their mums and
hold up paintings or collages of them. 'I love my Mum because . . .'.

3. Our mothers have lots of jobs to do and we should
help them as much as possible.

4. I keep the house clean.

Child wearing an apron, holding a feather duster, duster, tin of polish, etc.

5. I wash the clothes.

Child holding empty soap-powder packet and an item of clothing.

6. I iron the clothes.

Child mimes ironing, using the ironing-board from the home corner.

7. I cook the food.

Child holding a pan, if possible on a toy cooker.

8. I look after the baby.

Child gently rocking a doll.

POEM

This can be read by one child or by several children each reading one verse.

My Mum's a Supermum

My Mum's a supermum,
   She's really good to me.
She does so many different jobs
   And all of them for free.

She's always very sensible
   And does the best she can.
She cooks and cleans and nurses,
   And she's quite a handyman.

My Mum's a supermum,
   She's very kind and nice.
She always knows what's best to do,
   She's full of good advice.

She always goes on loving me,
   It's very, very true.
She's a supermum and no one else
   Could love her like I do.

9. My mother has another job.

Here, a selection of children whose mothers work outside the home can each say what his or her mum does and hold up a picture of the job. If possible, arrange for some mothers to come to the assembly and describe their jobs to the children.

10. Every year we have a special day
when we think of our mothers.

11. This is the fourth Sunday in Lent and
it is called Mother's Day.
Some people call it Mothering Sunday,
which is its proper name.

12. A long time ago children used to go away to work
and they were allowed a day off on Mothering Sunday
so that they could go home and visit their mothers.
They took spring flowers and Simnel cake
as special gifts.

Child holds up painting of cake.

13. Some people say that Simnel cake gets its name from
the legend of Simon and Nell.

PLAY

The Legend of Simon and Nell

Backdrop
A kitchen scene from many years ago – large open hearth with a wood fire; cooking
pot and utensils. This backdrop is not essential but, if you do provide it, you can
make use of it after the assembly. Let the children add collage pictures of the
characters, and use the finished scene as a display base for stories written by the
children.

Props

A table; bowls and spatulas for mixing; ingredients (empty packets of flour, raisins, marzipan).

Characters

Simon, Nell, narrator(s).

Costumes

You need 'peasant' clothes – a long skirt, simple blouse and apron for Nell; open-necked shirt or smock, knee-length trousers and socks for Simon.

Narrator Once there was a husband and wife. The husband was called Simon and the wife was called Nell. They were both good cooks but they were always quarrelling.

Nell I'm a better cook than you are.

Simon No, I'm the best cook. Men are always the best cooks.

Nell Your cooking always tastes horrible.

Simon No one ever tastes yours, because it always looks horrible.

Narrator   One day they decided to mix a cake
for Mothering Sunday.

Simon   Let's put in flour.
(As each ingredient is named, the children pretend to
mix them in the bowl.)

Nell   And fruit and eggs.

Simon   And some spices.

Narrator   They mixed up all the ingredients
in their bowls.

Simon   Let's boil it like a pudding.

Nell   That's silly. No one ever boils a cake,
we must bake it.

Simon   I'd like a boiled cake for a change.

Nell   Never! It has to be baked.

Narrator   They argued for a long time.
Then at last Nell said . . .

Nell   What if we boil it first and then bake it?

Simon   A good idea! Let's do it!

Narrator   At last the cake was finished and they
decorated it with round balls of marzipan.

Simon   We will put twelve balls on it.
One for Jesus and eleven for the Apostles.

Nell   Weren't there twelve Apostles?

Simon	We don't count Judas.

Simon and Nell	There, the cake is finished. Now we can celebrate Mothering Sunday.

14. The best gifts for Mother's Day are those things we do ourselves.

Children can stand and say what they will do for their mothers on Mother's Day.
For example:

I will make Mummy's bed.
I will help with the dishes.
I will help (Daddy) to make Mummy's breakfast.
I will do as I am told straight away.
I will keep my room tidy every day.

At the end of the assembly the children can stand and take their cards and gifts to their mothers or parents at the back. Take care to make provision for children whose mothers cannot attend.

SUMMER

BACKDROP

curtain or dark corrugated card, stapled to wall temporarily so that display can be removed to classroom

30 cm

green activity paper

CHECKLIST ▶

- Backdrop

- Children's seating arrangements

- Record-player

- Records: 'Summer' from *The Four Seasons* by Vivaldi or 'Morning' from the *Peer Gynt Suite* by Grieg. Cliff Richard singing 'We're all Going on a Summer Holiday'

- Cardboard sun

- Cardboard cloud

- Sunglasses and sunbathing clothes for one child

- Raincoat, umbrella and wellies for one child

- Swimwear, wellies and umbrellas for two children

- Easel or box with poster showing the names of the seasons and the same for the months May to August

- 'Glums' (paper faces) for the whole class

- Painting of flowers

- Painting of crops

- Picture of caterpillar or butterflies and paper butterflies to hold

- Five sunflower hats or masks

- Black tights and leotards for five children

- 'Hurray' flags for the whole class

- Four paintings of favourite summer activities and appropriate items, such as bucket and spade

29

- Sunglasses (children's own) for the whole class
- Card with the word 'danger' written on it
- Tube of protective cream for sunbathing
- Sunhat
- Nurse's uniform
- Empty containers for bicarbonate of soda and vinegar

- Swimming aids: armbands
- Card with the word 'drought' on it
- Card with the word 'famine' on it
- White dresses (for Whitsuntide)
- Poster of a maypole

TOPIC WEB ▶

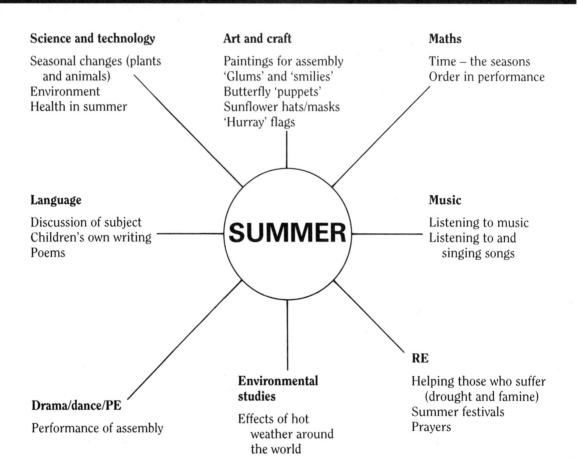

Science and technology
Seasonal changes (plants and animals)
Environment
Health in summer

Art and craft
Paintings for assembly
'Glums' and 'smilies'
Butterfly 'puppets'
Sunflower hats/masks
'Hurray' flags

Maths
Time – the seasons
Order in performance

Language
Discussion of subject
Children's own writing
Poems

SUMMER

Music
Listening to music
Listening to and singing songs

Drama/dance/PE
Performance of assembly

Environmental studies
Effects of hot weather around the world

RE
Helping those who suffer (drought and famine)
Summer festivals
Prayers

THE ASSEMBLY: Summer ▶

MUSIC

For entry into the assembly play 'Summer' from *The Four Seasons* by Vivaldi, or 'Morning' from the *Peer Gynt Suite* by Grieg.

1. Good morning.
Today we are going to talk about summer.

2. Sometimes it is very hot and sunny.

Child dressed in summer clothes and wearing sunglasses. Another child holds a cardboard sun up behind the first child.

3. Sometimes it is very wet.

Child dressed in raincoat with umbrella, which he or she opens. Another child holds up a cardboard cloud.

4. In this country there are four seasons in the year.

5. They are spring, summer, autumn and winter.

Child points to an easel (or box) on which there is a poster displaying the names of the seasons, with 'Summer' written in red to stand out.

6. The summer months are May, June, July and August.

Child points to a display similar to that for the seasons.

7. Summer usually has the warmest, dryest weather. The days are longer so we can play outside later.

POEM

Let one child read each verse. They should be dressed in swimwear with wellies and carrying open umbrellas.

Summer's hot, summer's cool,
Why is it I feel a fool?
Is it because this summer's day
I'm wearing wellies when I play?

I wouldn't really feel the same,
If I was playing out in rain.
But now I'm so hot when I run
'Cos for a change, there's lots of sun!

8. I don't like going to bed when it's light and sunny on a summer evening.

9. Neither do we!

The whole class says this, holding up 'glums' made from paper plates. Each child's 'glum' is decorated to look like him or her, and is held in front of the face. Later, they can be used to mount children's writing about summer bedtimes or other things they don't like in summer. Happy faces – 'smilies' – can be made as mounts for writing about more positive feelings about summer.

writing on reverse — crepe strip to ceiling

0. Summer is the time when everything grows quickly.

1. Flowers and plants grow in our gardens.

Child holds up painting of flowers or of a garden.

2. Crops grow in the farmers' fields.

Child holds up painting of countryside or of crops.

3. There are lots of insects like butterflies and caterpillars, and lots of busy birds eating them.

Child could hold up a picture of butterflies or of a huge caterpillar; or the class could make butterfly 'puppets' and a few children could flutter them at this point.

4. Sunflowers are the biggest flowers that people can grow in their gardens. Here is a poem about them.

POEM

The whole class can say this, or a group of six children. Five others act as sunflowers: they stand at the front and 'wilt' one at a time as the verse directs. These children wear sunflower hats/masks and either green clothes or black leotards and tights. Note that the fifth sunflower does not wilt but stretches out its arms in the sun.

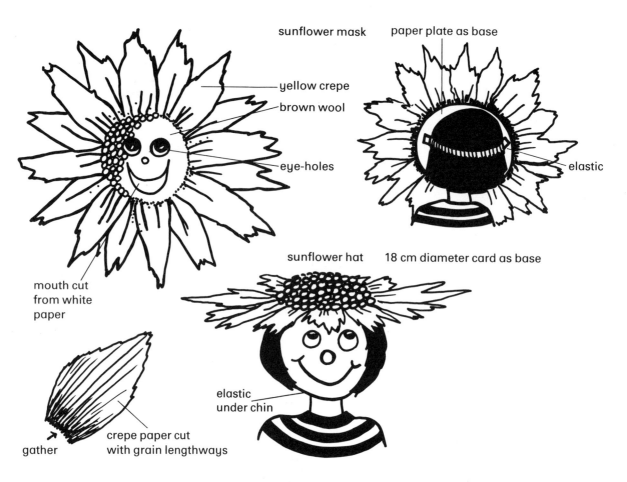

sunflower mask

paper plate as base

yellow crepe

brown wool

eye-holes

elastic

mouth cut
from white
paper

sunflower hat

18 cm diameter card as base

elastic
under chin

gather

crepe paper cut
with grain lengthways

Five little sunflowers grew in a row,
One had no water
So that didn't grow.

Four little sunflowers grew in a row,
One was too hot
So that didn't grow.

Three little sunflowers grew in a row,
A caterpillar ate one
So that didn't grow.

Two little sunflowers grew in a row,
The wind bent one
So that didn't grow.

One little sunflower grew all alone.
Soon she was the biggest
Little flower in town.

15. Summer is the time when we have the longest school holiday.

16. Hurray!

The whole class says this and each child can wave a flag.

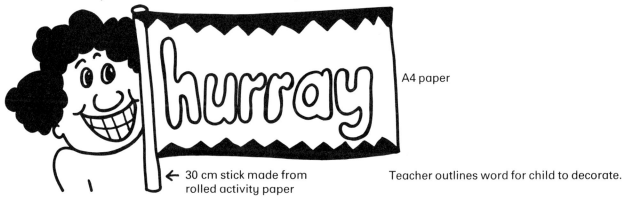

A4 paper

← 30 cm stick made from rolled activity paper

Teacher outlines word for child to decorate.

17. Lots of people go on holidays, trips and picnics in the summer.

18. Here are some of the things we like to do. Some hobbies and pastimes are just for summer-time.

Choose three or four children to say, or read out, what they have written about their favourite activity. For example:

I like to play in my paddling pool.
I like to go fishing with my Mum and Dad.
I like to play in the sea and on the sand.

They can hold up their own drawings or paintings or an item of the equipment they use, e.g. rubber ring, fishing-rod, bucket and spade.

19. Here is a poem about the seaside.

One or two children can read this poem by Robert Louis Stevenson.

***

POEM

***

At the Seaside

When I was down beside the sea
A wooden spade they gave to me
To dig the sandy shore.

My holes were empty like a cup,
In every hole the sea came up
Till it could come no more.

SONG

At this point the whole class could sing 'Oh, I do like to be beside the Seaside' by John Glover-Kind, from *Ta-ra-ra Boom-de-ay*, published by A. & C. Black. While the introduction is played on the piano, or the opening line on a xylophone or glockenspiel, the children each produce and put on a pair of sunglasses.

20. Summer can be dangerous too.

Child holds up a large sign with the word 'danger' on it in red.

21. You might get burnt by the sun, so use a cream to protect your skin.

Child holds up well-known brand of cream.

22. You might get sunstroke, which gives you a bad headache and sickness. So wear a sunhat or play in the shade.

Child puts on a sunhat.

23. You may get stung by a bee or a wasp.

24. If you are stung by a bee, mix some bicarbonate of soda into a paste and dab it on the sting.

Child wearing a nurse's uniform.

25. If you are stung by a wasp, dab vinegar on the sting and it will feel better.

This child also wears a nurse's uniform.

26. There's danger if you play near water, so stay away. If you can't swim, wear armbands when you go in the sea.

Child wears armbands.

27. Summer is a time for being happy and celebrating. We have festivals.

28. On Whit Sunday, people who belong to
a Christian church go on the Whit walk.
They walk around their parish in a big procession.

29. Many people wear white, for goodness.
That's why the day is called White Sunday, or Whitsun.
It is usually in May.

30. People want to show that they belong to the church.

For 27 to 30, the children could wear white clothes, if they have them.

31. The 1st of May is May Day. A long time ago,
people dressed up, decorated themselves with flowers
and danced around a maypole, to celebrate
the coming of summer.

Child holds up a picture of a maypole or garland of paper flowers.

32. In Russia, thousands of people parade in Red Square
in Moscow. They are celebrating freedom.

33. In parts of some countries, like Africa, South America
and Australia, it is summer nearly all the year round.

34. Sometimes it is so hot that all the water dries up and there is no rain. That is called a drought.

Child holds up card with the word 'drought' on it.

35. When it is too hot and dry, crops won't grow.
Then people do not have enough food.
That is called famine.

Child holds up card with the word 'famine' on it.

36. Lots of people die when there's a drought or famine.

37. We are very lucky because we don't get them in our country.

38. Let's say thank you.

PRAYER

---

39. Hands together, eyes closed.

All the children say the prayer.

Thank you for the long summer days
and the fun we have.
Thank you for the gifts of food
and water and happiness.

Amen

SONG

Choose one of these hymns or songs for the whole school to sing to finish the assembly:

'Abundantly' from *Alleluya*, published by A. & C. Black.

'Summer's Really Here' from *Every Colour Under the Sun*, published by Ward Lock Educational.

'I've seen the Golden Sunshine', 'I Love the Sun', 'Morning has Broken', all from *Someone's Singing, Lord*, published by A. & C. Black.

As music for the children to go out to, play Cliff Richard singing 'We're all Going on a Summer Holiday'.

FAMILY

BACKDROP

2 m card base

A large cottage is required, with many windows. This will serve both as the Three Bears' house and as a base for a display of work about the family. Each window is cut on three sides to make a flap, and a child's story is mounted inside.

CHECKLIST

- Backdrop

- Children's seating arrangements

- Record-player

- Record: 'He's got the Whole World in His Hands'

- Painting of a family

- Six paintings of family members

- Teapot and coffee jug or paintings of these

- Picture of mum cooking or pan to hold

- Picture of dad shopping or bag to hold

- Picture of child making bed or pillow to hold

- Picture of child washing car or bucket to hold

- Play: *Goldilocks and the Three Bears*
  props: three bear masks, three pillows and covers, three spoons and bowls, three chairs, one table

- Doll in blanket

- Picture of the royal family

- Collection of dolls for the 'Old Woman'

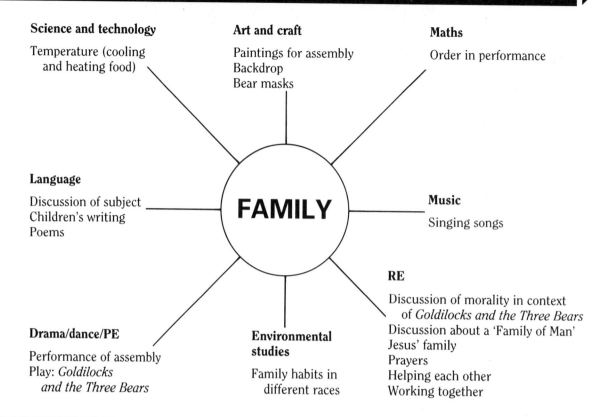

Science and technology

Temperature (cooling
and heating food)

Art and craft

Paintings for assembly
Backdrop
Bear masks

Maths

Order in performance

Language

Discussion of subject
Children's writing
Poems

FAMILY

Music

Singing songs

RE

Discussion of morality in context
of *Goldilocks and the Three Bears*
Discussion about a 'Family of Man'
Jesus' family
Prayers
Helping each other
Working together

Drama/dance/PE

Performance of assembly
Play: *Goldilocks
and the Three Bears*

**Environmental
studies**

Family habits in
different races

THE ASSEMBLY: Family ▶

MUSIC

For entry into the assembly, play 'He's got the Whole World in His Hands', which is
available on several folk records.

SONG

The whole school could sing 'Magic Penny' from *Alleluya*, published by A. & C. Black.

1. Good morning everybody. Our assembly
   is about families.

2. Families are people who love and care for each other
   and stay together.

3. Families are very special. We have a family at home.
   This is my family.

Child holds up picture of own family.

4. We've written about the people in our families and why we love them.

If each child writes about one person in the family, you can choose about six to present a passage each on one of the main relationships, i.e. with mum, dad, siblings, grandparent, etc. In this way, children without mother or without father can choose without fear of being left out. Examples:

I love Mummy because she looks after me.
I love my brother because he is funny and plays with me.

Each child holds up a large portrait of the person they are talking about.

5. Here is a poem about Gran and Grandad.

POEM

Two children can recite a verse each, with appropriate actions.

spectacles

Here are Grandma's spectacles,
Here is Grandma's hat,
Here's the way she folds her hands
And puts them in her lap.

hats

Here are Grandad's spectacles,
Here is Grandad's hat,
Here's the way he folds his arms
And takes a little nap.

6. Families sometimes argue a little . . . just a little.

7. Here is a nursery rhyme about this.

Two children say alternate lines, standing, hands on hips, facing each other, with cross faces. One holds a teapot and the other a coffee jug (or cut-out paintings of these things).

Molly, my sister, and I fell out
And what do you think it was all about?
She loves coffee and I love tea
And that's the reason we couldn't agree.

8. Knock, knock.   9. Who's there?

8. Yerbig.   9. Yerbig who?

8. Yerbig brother!

10. *(Mum)* Did you fall over with your new trousers on?

11. *(Son)* Yes Mum, but there wasn't time to take them off.

12. What's brown, hairy, has no legs, but walks? *(Waits)* Dad's socks!

13. There are lots of jobs to do when people live together.

14. Mum cooks the meals.

Child holds up a picture or a pan.

15. Dad does the shopping.

Child holds up a picture or a bag.

16. I make my bed.

Child holds up a picture or a pillow.

17. My brother/sister cleans the car.

Child holds up a picture or a bucket.

For 14 to 17, choose children whose relatives actually do the jobs mentioned, or use other examples the children think of.

18. We all work together to make our home.

19. Here is a story about a family who got everything ready and someone else spoiled it.

PLAY

Goldilocks and the Three Bears

Props
Three chairs; three pillows and bedcovers; three bowls and spoons; a table. If there is room, the scene can be set before the assembly starts; if not, the narrator and other children can quickly set things out.

Characters
Goldilocks, Mummy Bear, Daddy Bear, Baby Bear, narrator. The narrator could be the teacher, or the part could be shared between three children.

Costumes
The children can wear their usual clothes but the bears wear masks. Goldilocks should have blond hair or a blond wig.

stiff yellow art paper / felt-pen features

paper curls

cut holes

card strip is headband

25 cm

Stick on paper bow tie.

Enter Goldilocks, miming actions.

Narrator 1   A little girl called Goldilocks got lost in the woods.

Narrator 2   She found a little cottage and went inside.

Narrator 3   She saw three bowls of porridge on the table and tried them all.

Goldilocks   *(Trying each bowl)* Too hot. Too cold. Just right! *(She eats)*

Narrator 1   She saw three chairs and she tried them too. One broke.

Goldilocks	*(Trying each chair)* Too hard. Too soft. Just right. Ooops! *(Chair has broken. Child mimes.)*
Narrator 2	She saw three beds and she tried them too.
Goldilocks	*(Trying each bed)* Too lumpy. Too bouncy. Just right! *(She lies down to sleep.)* Zzzzzz.
Narrator 3	Just then the Three Bears, who owned the house, came home.
Daddy Bear	*(Looking at bowls)* Who's been eating my porridge?
Mummy Bear	And who's been eating my porridge?
Baby Bear	Who's been eating my porridge and has eaten it all up? Boo hoo!
Daddy Bear	*(Looking at chairs)* Who's been sitting on my chair?
Mummy Bear	And who's been sitting on my chair?
Baby Bear	Who's been sitting on my chair and broken it? Boo hoo!
Daddy Bear	*(Looking at beds)* Who's been lying on my bed?
Mummy Bear	And who's been lying on my bed?
Baby Bear	Who's been lying on my bed and is still in it? Boo hoo!

Narrator 1   Goldilocks woke up and ran away
as fast as she could. The Three Bears,
who looked after their home
so carefully, were very cross.

20. Baby Bear was so upset, I expect he had to have
a big cuddle before he went to bed that night.

21. Babies like lullabies to send them to sleep.
Here is a nice one.

22. Child rocks doll in his or her arms and looks down at it as he or she speaks.

Golden slumbers kiss your eyes,
Smiles await you when you rise.
Sleep, pretty baby, do not cry
And I will sing a lullaby.
Rock them, rock them, lullaby.

This is an alternative lullaby.

Rock-a-bye baby, thy cradle is green,
Father's a nobleman, Mother's a queen.
Betty's a lady and wears a gold ring,
And Johnny's a drummer and drums for the King.

23. We have a royal family in Britain.
The Queen is the Mum, and Prince Philip is the Dad.

24. It's a good thing we don't all have a family like this.

25. Child holds as many dolls as possible, from the home corner and home as well, if
necessary. Tie small dolls round the child's waist and to his or her arms.

There was an old woman who lived in a shoe,
She had so many children she didn't know what to do.
She gave them some broth without any bread,
Whipped them all soundly and sent them to bed.

26. We learnt a song about families.
    Did you know that we all have three families?

27. We belong to our family at home.

28. We are all a family at school because
    we all help each other and care for each other.

29. All the people in the world could be one big family.
    Then there would be no more fighting or wars.

SONG

This is sung by the class – or the whole school – to the tune of 'Sing a Song of Sixpence'.

The Family

Here we are together
    A happy family.
Boys and girls and teachers,
    Happy as can be.
Working hard and sharing,
    Having lots of fun.
Never ever giving up
    Until our work is done.

Here we are together
    A happy family.
Mum and Dad and children
    Happy as can be.
Sometimes there is laughter,
    Sometimes there are frowns,
But families should stick together
    Through their ups and downs.

Here we are together,
   The family of man.
People of all nations
   Must do the best they can.
If you can love your neighbour
   Whatever creed or kind,
Love and peace and friendship
   Are never hard to find.

PRAYER

Dear God,
Help us to share our lives together,
and love and care for our families.

                Amen

SIGNS AND SIGNALS

BACKDROP

CHECKLIST

- Backdrop

- Children's seating arrangements

- Record-player

- Records: 'Raindrops keep falling on my Head' by Burt Bacharach and 'Singing in the Rain' sung by Gene Kelly

- Four paintings of facial expressions: happy, sad, surprised, angry

- Three pictures/paintings to illustrate jobs: policeman or policewoman, musical conductor, airport signalman or signalwoman

- Two paintings: light clouds and rain clouds

- Four paintings of the seasons

- Pictures of different animal tracks

- Lollipop lady's or lollipop man's sign

- Pictures of different road signs

- Painting of warning lights around road works

- Traffic-lights (painting or model)

- Model of lighthouse (or painting)

- Painting of American Indian sending smoke signals

- A tom-tom

- Tape-recorder

- Tape of fire-engine, police car and ambulance sirens

- Play: *Noah's Ark*
    backdrop
    props: blue or green crepe paper, small branch, large rainbow
    nativity-style costumes, animal masks (and costumes if possible)

TOPIC WEB ▶

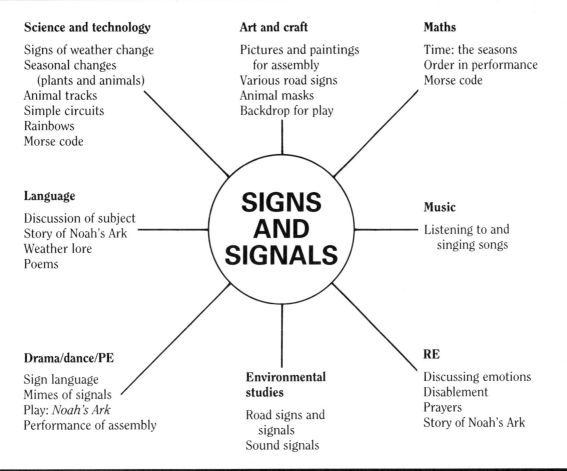

Science and technology

Signs of weather change
Seasonal changes
    (plants and animals)
Animal tracks
Simple circuits
Rainbows
Morse code

Art and craft

Pictures and paintings
    for assembly
Various road signs
Animal masks
Backdrop for play

Maths

Time: the seasons
Order in performance
Morse code

Language

Discussion of subject
Story of Noah's Ark
Weather lore
Poems

SIGNS AND SIGNALS

Music

Listening to and
    singing songs

Drama/dance/PE

Sign language
Mimes of signals
Play: *Noah's Ark*
Performance of assembly

Environmental studies

Road signs and
    signals
Sound signals

RE

Discussing emotions
Disablement
Prayers
Story of Noah's Ark

THE ASSEMBLY: Signs and signals ▶

MUSIC

For entry into the assembly, play 'Raindrops Keep Falling on my Head' by Burt Bacharach (this can be found in *Alleluya*, published by A. & C. Black); or 'Singing in the Rain', sung by Gene Kelly.

1. Good morning everybody. Welcome to our assembly. It is all about looking for signs and signals.

A hymn can be sung here, by the class or whole school.

2. We use our eyes to see things, but what we see depends upon how hard we look.

3. Faces sometimes show how people feel.

Child points to different pictures of faces.

This face is happy.
This face is sad.
This face is surprised.
This face is angry.

POEM

This poem can be recited either by a group of children or by the whole class.

My Face

My face is very special,
It belongs to only me,
And it can tell without a word
Exactly how I feel.

If tears are falling from my eyes
It tells you I am sad,
And if my face is all screwed up,
It means I'm feeling mad.

Then if my eyes are open wide
And if my mouth is too,
It means I'm really quite surprised
'Cos someone just said "Boo"!

But if I'm really happy,
As I am once in a while,
Then everybody knows because
I wear a great big smile.

4. People who cannot speak or hear use sign language. People who work in very noisy places use signs as well. We can use simple signs to tell these children what to do.

Here one child gives these signals to a group of four others, who do the appropriate actions.

A Come

B Stop

C Sit down

D Stand up

E Turn round

F Go back to your places

5. Sometimes people use signals in their jobs. Policemen and women use hand signals to stop traffic.

Child holds up a picture (or wears a police hat and signals with his or her arms).

6. A conductor uses arm and hand signals to conduct an orchestra.

Child holds up a picture (or wears a bow tie and waves a baton).

7. At an airport there are people who guide aeroplanes into "parking" places where the passengers get off.

Child holds up a picture (or wears ear muffs and holds up air control batons).

8. Signs in the sky tell us what the weather is like.
   Fair-weather clouds are light and fluffy.

   Child holds up a picture.

   Rain-clouds are dark and heavy.

   Child holds up a picture.

9. Here are two poems about the weather.

POEMS

These can be said either by a group of children or by the whole class.

Red sky at night, shepherds' delight.
Red sky in the morning, sailors' warning.

Whether the weather be fine,
Or whether the weather be not;
Whether the weather be cold,
Or whether the weather be hot;
We'll weather the weather,
Whatever the weather,
Whether we like it or not.

10. There are lots of signs in nature. We can see
    the seasons change by looking at flowers, trees
    and birds. The seasons are:

11. Spring.

    Child holds up a picture of spring.

12. Summer.

    Child holds up a picture of summer.

13. Autumn.

Child holds up a picture of autumn.

14. Winter.

Child holds up a picture of winter.

15. We can sometimes see animal tracks on the ground, too.

Several children each hold up a picture of animal tracks.

From the tracks we can find out if the animal was big or little, whether it walked or ran, and if it ran after another animal.

16. We see lots of signs on roads in town.
They give us information and tell us which way to go.
They warn us to watch out for things.
Signs help us to cross the road.
The lollipop man or lady holds up this sign to help us.

Child holds up cardboard sign.

At this stage a selection of other cardboard road signs could be held up.

17. Lights can give signals too.
Road works have yellow warning lights all around them.

Child holds up a painting (or perhaps a real light could be borrowed).

18. Traffic-lights control the cars, buses and lorries.

Child holds up a painting or model traffic-lights.

19. Lighthouses warn ships to keep clear of rocks.

Child holds up model lighthouse, or painting.

20. We can send messages using lights or sounds.
This is called Morse code.
American Indians used to send smoke signals.

Child holds up picture of smoke signals.

21. African tribes used to send messages on their drums.

Child could beat out a rhythm on a tom-tom drum.

22. Sometimes sounds are used to give warnings
and signals.

Play a tape-recording of fire-engine, police car and ambulance sirens.

23. Fire-engines, police cars and ambulances all make
a lot of noise when they are in a hurry to get to
a fire, a robbery or an accident.

24. Burglar alarms help to protect our houses and shops.
We use a bell to tell us when to come into school.
A referee uses a whistle to control a football match.
We need alarm-clocks to wake us up in the mornings.

Child rings bell or blows a whistle.

25. There are lots of other signs and signals all around us.
Some we can see very easily, but to see the others
we have to look very carefully.

POEM

This can be recited by a group of children, taking parts or all together; or by the whole class.

Signs

Whenever I can find the time
I like to look around for signs.
In the countryside I see
The signs that nature gives to me.
If a cloudy sky is grey
It means another rainy day;
And when you hear a cuckoo sing,
They say that it's a sign of spring.
From tracks upon the ground I know
The animals that come and go.
Just what these signs all say to me
Depends on what I try to see.

There are lots and lots of signs in town
On walls, on lamp-posts, on the ground.
They warn us and inform us too.
They always tell us what to do.
Some tell us not to drive too fast,
And others say "Keep off the grass"!
Shop windows and their signs all tell
The kind of shop and what they sell.
And on the railways, signals show
The trains when they should stop and go.
My hands can wave to all my friends
To say goodbye this is:
The End

PLAY

If a play is included, the following one about Noah's Ark might be suitable, since at the end there is a sign from God – the rainbow – to show there will never be another flood like that.

Noah's Ark

Backdrop
A picture of the Ark is painted on a large piece of corrugated card. Two large sheets of paper are folded back as shown, so that the pictures of the trees reveal the Ark.

Fix back sheet to display boards, 2 easels or the wall to give security.

1½ m

2 m

Children to open when needed.

Props
Roll of blue or green crepe paper; a small branch; a large cardboard rainbow; shepherds' crooks.

Characters
Narrators 1, 2, 3 and 4,   God's voice,   Noah,   Noah's wife,   Noah's family (number not fixed), neighbours (three of whom speak),   the Dove,   pairs of animals.

Costumes
Nativity-style costumes for the people. Animal masks and suitable clothes for the pairs of animals, or the children can paint large pictures of the animals and hold them in front of them.

Noah and his family are working in the fields and looking after sheep.

Narrator 1   In the Bible there are lots of stories about signs from God. One of these stories is about Noah and his Ark.

Narrator 2   Noah lived with his family and did his best to be good and kind. One day he had a message from God.

God's voice   Noah, I am going to make it rain. You must build a big boat and take your family and two of every kind of creature on board.

Noah goes to his family.

Noah   Come on, everybody! We must build a big boat. Soon it will start to rain and there will be a flood. We will be safe if we make the ship strong enough.

Noah and his family start to build the Ark. The children mime sawing, hammering, carrying. A group of neighbours enters, hands over ears, and goes to speak to Noah.

1st neighbour   What are you doing, Noah?

Noah   I'm building an ark.
There is going to be a flood,
and I will save all the animals
and my family too.

2nd neighbour   Who says there's going to be a flood?
It's a lovely sunny day.
We are going on a picnic.
It's much too nice to work.

Noah's wife   You had better build a boat too
or else you will drown.

3rd neighbour   We are not wasting our time
when we could be having fun.

All the neighbours laugh at Noah and walk away.

Noah's wife   You'll be sorry.

Narrator 3   At last the boat is ready.

The picture of the trees is opened to reveal the Ark.

Noah   Now we are ready. Go out and find
two of every kind of creature,
a male and a female.

The family of Noah gathers in all the animals, who come on stage in twos and group together to sing 'Who Built the Ark', from Come and Sing, published by A. & C. Black.

Narrator 3   Suddenly it starts to rain. It rains
and it rains, and it starts to flood.

To suggest rising water, waft an opened roll of crepe paper up and down.

All neighbours   Help! Help! Save us, we're drowning.

Noah   There is nothing we can do.

Narrator 4   The rain goes on for days and days.
Noah and his family and all
the animals are safe.
At last the rain stops.

Noah   Come here, Dove. Go out and see
if you can find any land.

The Dove 'flies' off and returns with a branch in its mouth.

Noah   Look! It is a sign that the water
is going down.

The Dove 'flies' off.

Noah's wife   Look! What is that in the sky?
(She points to a rainbow.)

Noah   That is a rainbow. It is God's way of
saying that it will never rain like that
again. Let us say a prayer
to thank God for saving us.

All   Dear God, we thank you for
bringing us safely through
the dangers of the flood.
Amen

All stand and sing 'Sing a Rainbow' *from* Apusskidu, *published by A. & C. Black.*

To end the assembly, the whole school could sing 'Rise and Shine' or 'Abundantly', both
from *Alleluya*, published by A. & C. Black.

AIR

BACKDROP

CHECKLIST

- Backdrop

- Children's seating arrangements

- Record-player

- Records: 'Let's go Fly a Kite' from *Mary Poppins* and 'Up, Up and Away in my Beautiful Balloon'

- Picture of two kinds of windmill

- Picture of yacht

- Large paper fan

- Collage of washing on a line

- Picture or poster of a mountaineer

- Picture or poster of a spaceman

- Picture or poster of a deep-sea diver

- Bicycle

- Picture or poster of a hovercraft or a toy hovercraft

- Picture or poster of a monorail or a toy monorail

- Two sheets of paper

- A toy parachute or one made from a handkerchief

- Transparent tank containing water

- Balloons (at least one inflated)

- Plastic tube

- Plastic bottle

- Ping-pong ball

- Glass jar

- Candle and matches (teacher only)

- Paper gliders and aeroplanes

- Bubble prints

- Paint-blot pictures (blown with a straw)

- Play: *The Sun and the Wind*
  props: large faces of the sun and wind
  costume for traveller: warm coat, scarf
  and hat on top; T-shirt and shorts
  underneath; sunglasses

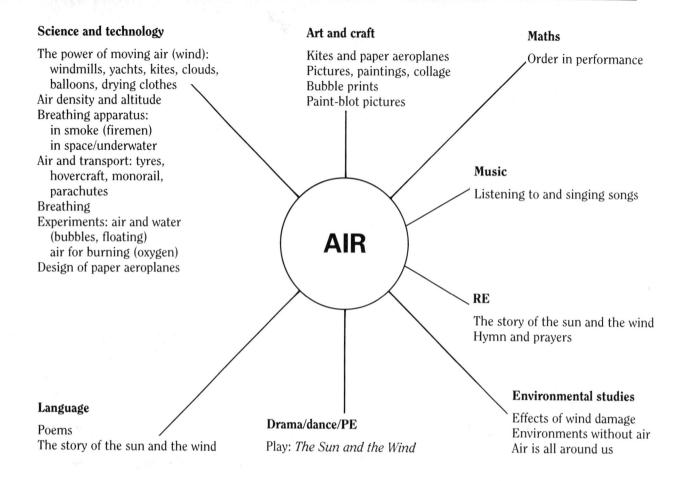

Science and technology

The power of moving air (wind):
    windmills, yachts, kites, clouds,
    balloons, drying clothes
Air density and altitude
Breathing apparatus:
    in smoke (firemen)
    in space/underwater
Air and transport: tyres,
    hovercraft, monorail,
    parachutes
Breathing
Experiments: air and water
    (bubbles, floating)
    air for burning (oxygen)
Design of paper aeroplanes

Art and craft

Kites and paper aeroplanes
Pictures, paintings, collage
Bubble prints
Paint-blot pictures

Maths

Order in performance

Music

Listening to and singing songs

AIR

RE

The story of the sun and the wind
Hymn and prayers

Language

Poems
The story of the sun and the wind

Drama/dance/PE

Play: *The Sun and the Wind*

Environmental studies

Effects of wind damage
Environments without air
Air is all around us

THE ASSEMBLY: Air ▶

1. Good morning everyone. Our assembly is all about air.

   A hymn can be sung here, for example 'God made the Sun'.

2. Air is all around us. We cannot see it but we can feel it. Blow on your fingers.

   Everyone blows on their fingers.

3. Moving air is called wind, and lots of things use the power of wind to make them move.

4. A windmill's sails are turned by moving air. Windmills can be used for grinding corn or to make electricity.

   Child holds up posters or own painting of two different windmills.

5. Yachts have large sails to catch the wind.
   They make the yacht move through the water.

6. The wind can be gentle and it keeps us cool
   on a hot day.

7. If there is no wind, we can make a fan.
   By waving it to and fro like this,
   we can cool ourselves.

   Child waves a large paper fan.

8. Wind helps to dry clothes on the washing line.

   Child points to collage.

9. When it is windy we can have fun flying kites.
   We made some kites in class.

   Child points to backdrop.

10. On a windy day we see clouds racing across the sky.

   Child points to backdrop.

SONG

At this stage the class could sing 'Kite Song' from *Silly Aunt Sally*, published by Ward Lock Educational.

11. Wind can cause a lot of damage if it blows too hard.
    Houses can be damaged and trees can be blown over.

POEM

Each verse is read by a different child, holding a kite, toy windmill or yacht, or waving a fan, as appropriate.

12. What can toss my kite so high,
    And blow hats all around?
    What dries the washing on the line
    And knocks trees to the ground?

13. What can make the windmills turn?
    Round and round they go.
    If it blows hard they go round fast,
    If gently they go slow.

14. The sails of yachts are filled with this
    As they go sailing by.
    Heat it up and fill balloons,
    They rise into the sky.

15. We need fresh air so we can breathe,
    Without it there's no sound.
    It's there but it's invisible,
    Yet wind is all around.

16. There is a lot of air close to the Earth's surface,
    but as we go higher there is less and less air.

17. At the top of very high mountains there is very little air
    and it is hard to breathe.

Child holds up picture of mountaineer.

18. In space there is no air at all and people need space suits with an air supply to keep them alive.

Child holds up a picture.

19. Divers carry an air supply with them so that they can breathe under water. The air is in cylinders on the diver's back.

Child holds up a picture.

20. Firemen wear breathing apparatus when the air is full of smoke.

If possible, child wears a toy fire-helmet and carries a small section of hose-pipe.

21. We can use air to help us to travel smoothly. Cars and bicycles have air in their tyres so that the ride is not bumpy.

Child shows bicycle to audience, and gently bounces it up and down.

22. A hovercraft uses a cushion of air so that it can travel smoothly over land or water.

Child holds up picture or model.

23. A monorail floats on a cushion of air. It can move very fast.

Child holds up picture or model.

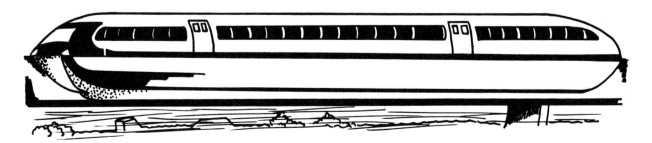

24. Air can hold things up.
Let's take two pieces of paper,
one flat and one screwed into a ball,
and let them both fall from the same height.

Child drops a ball of paper and a flat sheet.

25. The flat sheet falls more slowly because
more air is trapped underneath it.
The crumpled sheet falls quite quickly.

26. A parachute works in the same way.
It helps to slow down someone who has jumped from
an aeroplane, so that they don't get hurt.

Child holds up a picture of a parachutist or throws up a toy parachute. Alternatively
a simple parachute can be made, as shown.

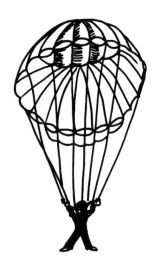
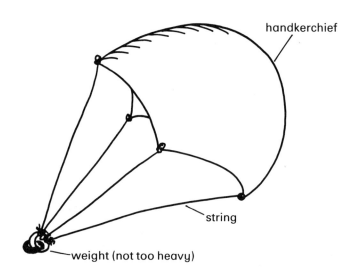

handkerchief

string

weight (not too heavy)

27. We need air to breathe through our lungs.
Our lungs are like two large balloons in our chest.

28. When we breathe in, our lungs get bigger.

All the children breathe in.

29. When we breathe out, our lungs go down.

All children breathe out.

30. We usually breathe fairly slowly.

31. When we run we need more air, so we breathe faster.

Child runs round the perimeter of the hall and returns, breathing fast.

32. Here are some experiments to show you that air is all around us. Here are the things we will use.

Child points to and names each item. The items are laid out on a table.

Transparent tank full of water
Plastic tube
Balloons
Ping-pong ball
Plastic bottle
Candle
Glass jar

At this stage, four children and the teacher take up positions beside the equipment for each of the five experiments. Each demonstrates the experiment about which he or she speaks. Note that one balloon must be blown up.

33. If we blow into the water through the plastic tube, we can see bubbles of air.

34. It is very hard to push the balloon under water, because the balloon is full of air and floats up, like the bubbles.

35. The ping-pong ball always floats to the surface of the water because it has air inside it.

36. When the top is on the bottle the water cannot get in and the bottle floats. *(Child takes top off bottle.)* When we take the top off, the water rushes in and the bottle starts to sink.

Note: The next and last experiment MUST BE DONE BY THE TEACHER.

37. *(Teacher)* A flame needs air to burn *(lights candle)*. This flame will go out when all the air in the jar has been used up *(places glass jar over candle)*.

38. We made some paper aeroplanes and we tested them to see which could fly furthest.

Children demonstrate their designs and then fly their planes along the line of the stage. They can be picked up by whoever is nearest and held until the end of the assembly.

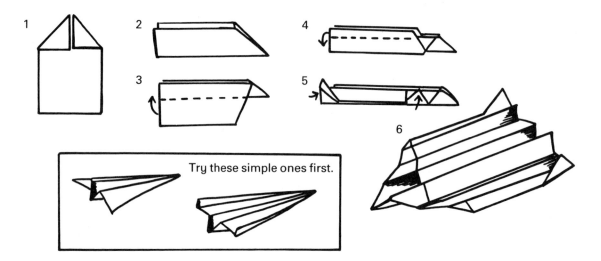

Try these simple ones first.

39. Air helps things move.

Child blows up balloon and lets it go.

When the air escapes it makes the balloon go forward very quickly.

40. We used air to make these pictures.

Child points to bubble prints and paint-blot pictures.

POEM

This can be recited by one or two children. At the end, the reader(s) could blow some bubbles with bubble mixture and a wire ring.

Bubbles from my pipe I blow,
Red, yellow in the air.
Orange, green, off they go,
Blue, white, everywhere.

Bubbles from my pipe I blow,
Pink, violet in the air,
Red and purple, off they go,
Rainbows everywhere.

PLAY

The Sun and the Wind

Characters
The sun, the wind, a traveller, a narrator.

Costumes
The children who play the sun and the wind hold large cardboard faces, as shown.
The traveller wears warm outdoor clothes over everyday clothes.

Narrator A traveller was walking down the road as the sun and the wind were having an argument.

Wind I am stronger than you.

Sun Never! I am much stronger than you.

Wind I can blow down trees and houses. You can't.

Sun I am strong in a different way.

Wind You are only saying that.

Sun Can you see that traveller? Well, whoever can make him take off his coat will be the stronger.

Wind That's too easy. I'll make him take off his coat right now. I'll blow it off!

67

Narrator   The wind blew and blew, but the traveller only pulled his coat round him and he would not take it off.
(Traveller does this.)

Sun   Now it's my turn.

Narrator   The sun chased all the dark clouds away and shone hot in the bright blue sky.

Traveller   Phew! It's suddenly gone very warm. I think I'll have to take off my coat.
(Traveller takes off coat.)

Narrator   The sun had won and the wind went off, sulking. The sun proved that kindness and gentleness are much better ways to persuade people than shouting and bullying.

41. Let's say our prayer together.

PRAYER

This is said by the whole class or whole school.

Thank you God for the air we breathe:
for the life it gives to all living creatures,
and for the cool breezes that softly blow,
and for the winds that bring us weather
to make crops grow.
        Amen

SONG

To finish the assembly, these songs could be sung by the class or by the whole school; or they could be played on the record-player as the children leave the hall: 'Up, Up and Away'; or 'Let's go Fly a Kite' from *Mary Poppins*.

FAVOURITE THINGS

BACKDROP

box outline painted

letters cut from activity paper

corrugated card stapled to wall temporarily

Our favourite things.

Class 6

Mum

Dad

Cut out children's own paintings.

stage blocks

CHECKLIST

- Backdrop

- Children's seating arrangements

- Record-player

- Record: 'My Favourite Things' from *The Sound of Music*

- Picture of eyes (sight)

- Picture of hands (touch)

- Picture of tongue (taste)

- Picture of ears (hearing)

- Picture of nose (smell)

- Painting of kitten and hot pan (or toy fluffy kitten and saucepan)

- Painting of ice-cream and large pie

- Painting of child listening to singing bird

- Painting of child sniffing flowers (or bunch of flowers)

- Selection of the children's favourite things

- Play: *King Midas and the Golden Touch*
  props: brocade curtain (or similar); chair and material for throne; table covered with similar material; corrugated paper; cups, plates and spoons covered with gold foil; gold mask; glockenspiel
  costumes: sheets for togas; white dress for Midas' daughter

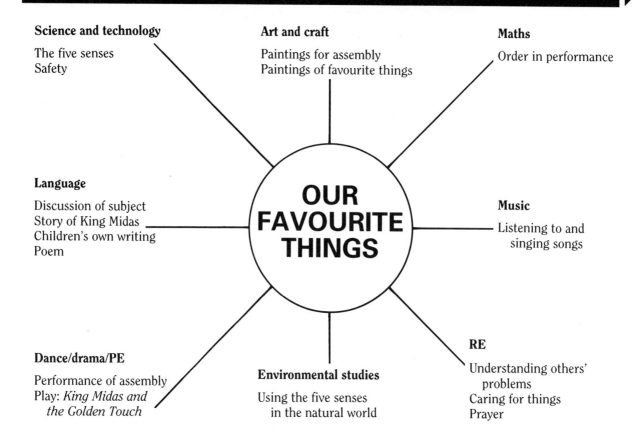

Science and technology

The five senses
Safety

Art and craft

Paintings for assembly
Paintings of favourite things

Maths

Order in performance

Language

Discussion of subject
Story of King Midas
Children's own writing
Poem

OUR FAVOURITE THINGS

Music

Listening to and
  singing songs

Dance/drama/PE

Performance of assembly
Play: *King Midas and
  the Golden Touch*

Environmental studies

Using the five senses
  in the natural world

RE

Understanding others'
  problems
Caring for things
Prayer

THE ASSEMBLY: Favourite things ▶

For entry into the assembly, play 'My Favourite Things' from *The Sound of Music*.

1. Good morning everybody. Welcome to our assembly. It is all about our favourite things.

2. We have five senses.

   Five children hold up appropriate pictures as the reader says the names of the senses.

   Sight.   Touch.   Taste.   Hearing.   Smell.

   Here, the class or whole school could sing a hymn or song such as 'He Gave Me Eyes So I Could See'; or 'Someone's Singing, Lord' from the book of the same name, published by A. & C. Black.

3. If we did not have sight, we would not be able to see the things around us.
   Blind people cannot see anything at all.
   It is dark all the time.

4. If we couldn't touch things, we wouldn't be able to feel the softness of a kitten's fur. We wouldn't know if we were being hurt by touching very hot things.

Child holds up painting or toy kitten and pan.

5. If we couldn't taste things, we wouldn't know how delicious it is to eat our favourite foods, like ice-cream or apple pie.

Child holds up painting.

6. If we couldn't hear, we would not be able to listen to music or to birds singing.

Child holds up painting.

7. We would have to use our hands to say things, as many deaf people do.
Deaf people live in a silent world.
This is "Hello" in the deaf and dumb language.

Child makes appropriate sign.

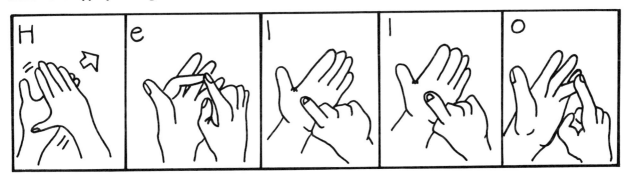

8. If we couldn't smell things we would not know the scent of flowers or the delicious smells of cooking.

SONG

Here the whole class sings the song 'My Favourite Things' from *The Sound of Music*.

After the song, four children read what they have written previously about their favourite things, and show pictures they have painted. Topics could include foods, TV programmes, books, toys, games, lessons, animals, places.

Then four other children each show something special that they have brought from home. Each says why the item is special (this can be read out from child's previously prepared written work; or the words can be memorised).

9. All things are precious to someone.
   We should care for other people's property.

POEM

One or two children can recite this, or a small group.

Mum and Dad

I really love my Mum and Dad,
But sometimes they can drive me mad.
They always send me off to bed
When I could watch TV instead.
Then next morning in they creep
And wake me when I'm still asleep.

It's "Keep your clothes clean now" and "Oh!
Who's made that mess upon the floor?
Wash your neck and clean your teeth
And don't forget your manners please."
It's hard remembering all of this,
Especially when you're only six.

10. Too much of a good thing is not always good for you.
    Here is what happened to someone
    who loved something so much that he wished
    everything he touched to turn into it.

PLAY

King Midas and the Golden Touch

Backdrop
This is not essential, but you could staple a brocade-type curtain to the wall and make a 'classical' pillar with a roll of corrugated paper.

Props
Chair and table, both covered with material to make a throne and royal table; cups, plates and spoons covered with gold metallic foil; gold mask (see illustration); glockenspiel and hard beater.

72

golden mask

Cut out face-shape and features from gold paper.

Strips of gold paper can be cut out and curled for the hair, or use gift-wrap ribbon curled by pulling it across one blade of a pair of scissors. Assemble the mask and glue onto a stick.

Characters
King Midas, stranger, King Midas's daughter, servants (non-speaking parts), six narrators.

Costumes
Use sheets as togas, and a simple white dress for the daughter.

Narrator 1	King Midas was the King of Greece. He loved gold very much. One day he was counting his gold.
King Midas	*(Mimes counting gold)* Oh, I love gold. It is so beautiful. I wish I had lots and lots of it.
Narrator 2	Just then a man came and spoke to the King.

Stranger enters and goes up to King Midas.

Stranger	Midas, are you sure that you love gold as much as that?
King Midas	Oh yes! I even wish that everything I touch would turn to gold.
Stranger	I can grant your wish if you are really sure.

73

King Midas   Yes, yes, yes. Do it now.

Sound of glissando on glockenspiel, to show the magic has worked.

Narrator 3   King Midas ran around
changing everything to gold.

King goes to the side and, with his back to the audience, picks up the gold objects and puts them on the table.

Narrator 3   After a while he got tired and sent for
his servants to bring him food.

Enter servants.

King Midas   *(To servants)* Bring me food and wine.

Servants bow and go out.

Narrator 4   The servants came in with food and wine
but as soon as King Midas touched it,
it turned to gold.

King Midas   *(Waving hand at table)*
Ugh! This is horrible.
I cannot eat it. Take it away.
(He sinks down onto his throne, tired out.)
I wish everything did not turn to gold.

Narrator 5   Suddenly his daughter, the Princess,
ran in. She looked at the golden things.

*Daughter runs in and looks at golden things on the table.
She picks up a golden spoon.*

Daughter   Oh Daddy, it's beautiful. Can I have this?
(She runs over to the King.)

King Midas   *(Drawing back)* Stop!

Daughter grabs his hand and turns into a statue, i.e. immediately stands still, holding gold mask over her face.

King Midas   Oh, no! She is a golden statue.

The stranger enters. King Midas rushes up to him.

King Midas   Oh, please take your gift back.
I hate the sight of gold!

Stranger   Go and wash in the river and then
come back. When you touch
the golden things they will
change back to normal.

Narrator 6   King Midas washed in the river.
When he returned to the palace
he changed everything back again.

King Midas touches his daughter, who immediately moves, drops the mask and smiles.

King Midas   *(Taking his daughter's hand)*
I will never wish for gold again.
I love the real flowers and birds
and my dear daughter. The only gold
I love is the gold of the sunshine.

SONG

To finish the assembly the class – or the whole school – could sing either 'I love the Sun' or 'Think of a World without any Flowers', both from *Someone's Singing, Lord*, published by A. & C. Black.

CLOTHES

BACKDROP

CHECKLIST

- Backdrop

- Children's seating arrangements

- Record-player

- Records: *Joseph and the Amazing Technicolour Dreamcoat* by Tim Rice and Andrew Lloyd Webber, or 'The King is in the Altogether' sung by Danny Kaye

- Chart showing different materials (cotton, wool, nylon, leather, rubber)

- Picture of a suit of armour

- Examples of children's weaving (paper or wool)

- Winter clothes for one child

- Waterproof clothes for one child

- Summer clothes for one child

- Pyjamas for one child

- Swimming costume for one child

- Football kit for one child

- Bridesmaid's dress for one child

- Collection of clothes for dressing up

- Clothes with zips (body warmer) and Velcro (trainers)

- Chart to show occupations requiring special clothing, plus job titles on cards

- Hats (police, fire-helmet, hard hat as used on building-site)

- Rubber diving suit or toy diver or picture

- Toy spaceman or illustration of spaceman

- National costumes: Scottish, Dutch, Welsh, Hawaiian (use illustrations, costume dolls or borrowed clothes)

- Play: *The King's New Clothes*
  props: chair with drape, table, hand mirror
  costumes: for the Prime Minister, use one of the costumes for the Three Kings in a Nativity play. The King wears white shorts and T-shirt or vest beneath a long shift/tunic (something easy to take off). He has a crown and a long cloak. The tailors and crowd wear peasant clothes.

TOPIC WEB ▶

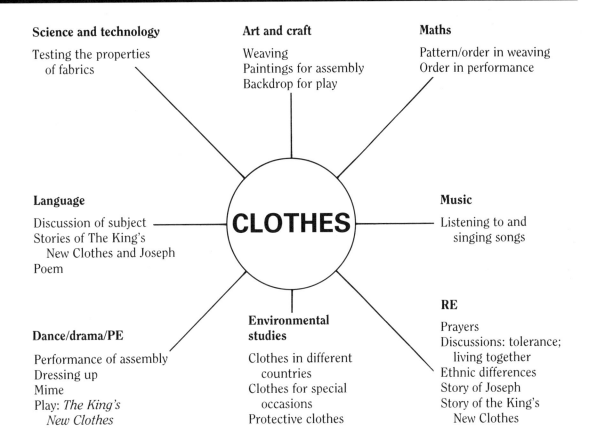

Science and technology

Testing the properties of fabrics

Art and craft

Weaving
Paintings for assembly
Backdrop for play

Maths

Pattern/order in weaving
Order in performance

Language

Discussion of subject
Stories of The King's New Clothes and Joseph
Poem

CLOTHES

Music

Listening to and singing songs

Dance/drama/PE

Performance of assembly
Dressing up
Mime
Play: *The King's New Clothes*

Environmental studies

Clothes in different countries
Clothes for special occasions
Protective clothes

RE

Prayers
Discussions: tolerance; living together
Ethnic differences
Story of Joseph
Story of the King's New Clothes

THE ASSEMBLY: Clothes ▶

For entry into the assembly play a song from *Joseph and the Amazing Technicolour Dreamcoat*, the musical by Tim Rice and Andrew Lloyd Webber.

1. Good morning everybody.
   Our assembly is all about clothes.

2. People wear clothes for many different reasons, sometimes to keep them warm, sometimes for protection, sometimes to show the kind of job they do, and sometimes to show what country they come from.

3. Clothes are made of different materials.
   They can be made of cotton, wool, nylon,
   leather, rubber or even metal!

Child points to chart of different materials and holds up picture of suit of armour.

4. Material for clothes is made by criss-crossing wool or
   cotton. This is called weaving.

5. We have been weaving with paper/wool
   and this is what we made.

Here, several children hold up examples of their paper weaving to show warp and
weft, or some wool weaving done on a carton loom.

Stick first row of warp to one
strip of weft, and the same with the last row.

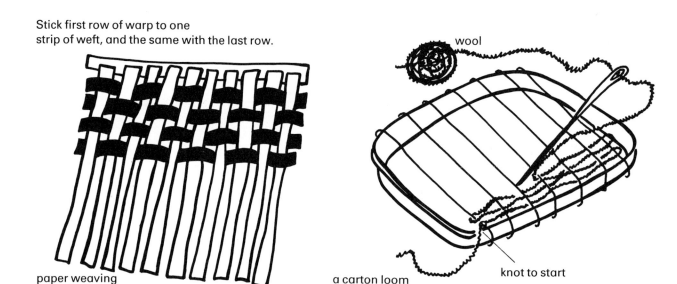

paper weaving   a carton loom

6. When it is winter we wear clothes that keep us warm.

Child is dressed in winter clothes – or could hold up picture.

7. When it is raining we wear waterproof clothes
   and wellingtons on our feet.

Child wears these clothes.

8. When it is hot we wear cotton clothes to keep us cool
   and sandals on our feet.

Child wears these clothes.

SONG

The whole class sings this song to the tune of 'There is a Tavern in the Town'.

Hats and coats and gloves and shoes,
   Gloves and shoes.
Hats and coats and gloves and shoes
   Gloves and shoes.
Snow and rain and sunshine help us choose
Hats and coats and gloves and shoes.

9. We wear different clothes for different occasions.

10. When I go to bed, I wear pyjamas.

Child wears pyjamas.

11. When I go swimming, I wear my swimming costume.

Child wears swimming costume.

12. When I play football, I wear my football kit.

Child wears football kit.

13. When I was a bridesmaid, I wore this dress.

If possible, child wears her own dress that she wore as a bridesmaid.

14. When I get up in the morning I can dress myself.

Two or three children in shorts, T-shirts and blouse or shirt with the top two buttons undone stand side by side. They say each of the following lines together, demonstrating each stage and treating it almost as a race (pick the quickest dressers!).

I can fasten buttons.

They fasten the top buttons on blouse or shirt. When everyone has done that . . .

I can put my jumper on.

They each sort out tangled sleeves and put on a jumper the right way round. When everyone has done that . . .

I can put my shoes on.

They fasten buckles or tie laces.

79

Now we are all dressed.

15. Some clothes can be fastened quickly.
Zips fasten quickly.

Child wears a body-warmer with a zip-fastener and zips it up.

16. Velcro fastens quickly too.

Child wears trainers and fastens Velcro tops, putting each foot on chair so that audience can see.

POEM

This can be said by one or two children or by the whole class.

I Can

I can tie my shoelace,
I can brush my hair,
I can wash my hands and face.
And dry myself with care.

I can clean my teeth too,
And fasten up my frock.
I can say, "How do you do",
And pull up both my socks.

17. People who do special jobs wear special clothes so we can recognise them.

Child points to backdrop. Six children are invited from the audience to put name cards next to the pictures.

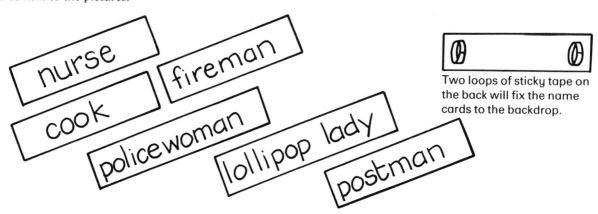

Two loops of sticky tape on the back will fix the name cards to the backdrop.

18. Sometimes people wear special clothes
    to protect themselves.

19. Policemen and women wear hard hats
    to protect their heads.

If possible, child shows police helmet or protective hat, or a picture of these.

20. Firemen have hard hats and they wear
    breathing masks when they go into
    a burning building full of smoke.

If possible, child shows fire-helmet, or a picture of one.

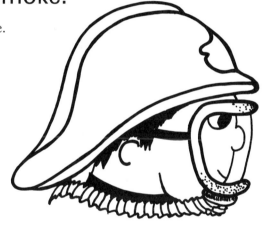

21. Building workers have hard hats, too, and steel-capped
    shoes in case bricks or wooden planks fall on them.

If possible, child shows hard hat, or a picture of one.

22. A diver needs an aqualung so that he or she can breathe under water, and a rubber suit to keep warm.

Child holds up rubber suit, or a toy diver, or a picture.

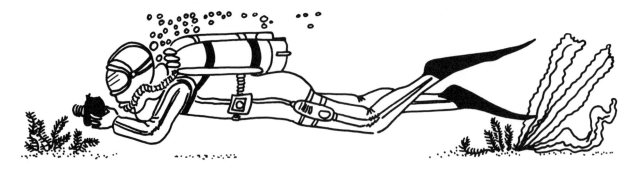

23. A spaceman has to wear a special suit. It protects him, keeps him warm and lets him breathe in space. Deep-sea divers wear suits like this too.

Child holds up toy spaceman or toy space suit, or a picture.

24. Some countries have a national costume. People wear it on special occasions.

To illustrate this section, use dolls in national costumes or a display of pictures, or children's own paintings. It may even be possible to borrow appropriate clothes.

25. This man is from Scotland.

26. This lady is from Holland.

27. Here is a Welsh lady.

28. This lady comes from Hawaii.

29. People have come from all over the world to live in Britain. Some of them wear clothes that are special to them.

If possible, invite Muslim, Sikh, Hindu and Chinese children, and/or their parents, to display their special clothes and talk about them. Perhaps they would loan items and help with a display, or a series of displays over a period of time.

30. Our play is about someone who loved clothes very much and how he was tricked. It is called *The King's New Clothes*.

If necessary at this stage, play a little music, for example, 'The King is in the Altogether' sung by Danny Kaye.

PLAY

The King's New Clothes

Backdrop
This could be as shown, or merely a chair covered with a drape, and a table.
The background could be plain.

Props
As above, plus a hand mirror.

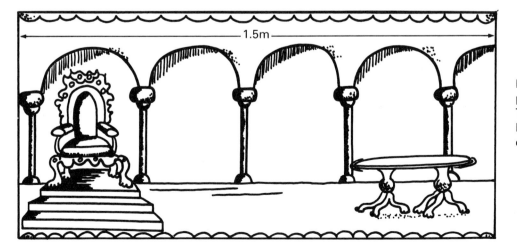

Paint palace scene on paper or card roll. Transfer to classroom later and add cut-out characters from play.

Characters

The King, the Prime Minister, two tailors, a little boy, the crowd (non-speaking parts), a narrator (the teacher).

Costumes

For the Prime Minister, use one of the costumes for the Three Kings in a Nativity play. The King wears white shorts and T-shirt or vest beneath a long shift/tunic (something easy to take off). He has a crown and a long cloak. The tailors and crowd wear peasant clothes.

King	*(Looking in mirror)* I am the most handsome King in all the world. I am very smart in my new clothes.

Two tailors enter.

Both tailors	May we make you a new suit, Your Majesty?
King	Oh, yes! I will need a new suit for the Grand Parade.
Tailor 1	We will need ten bags of gold to buy some special magic material.
King	How is it magic?
Tailor 2	Well, only clever people can see the cloth.
King	Good. I will be able to see who is really clever. Here is the gold. *(Mimes giving bags of gold)* Start straight away.

The tailors go over to the table at the side of the stage and pretend to cut out and sew.

Narrator	The two tailors went away to make the special suit. Three days later the King called for the Prime Minister.

Prime Minister enters.

84

PM   Yes, Your Majesty?

King   Go and see how my new suit is coming along. It should be ready by now.

Prime Minister goes over to the two tailors.

Narrator   The Prime Minister went to the tailors. Of course, he could see nothing but he wouldn't admit it.

PM   It's so beautiful!
I must go and tell the King.
(He rushes back to the King.)
Your Majesty, it is the most wonderful suit I have ever seen.
It will be just right for the Parade.

Narrator   The King sent more people to look at the suit. They all agreed that it was really beautiful because no one wanted to be thought stupid.

Several single people and pairs (members of the crowd) come in, look at the table, and nod and smile to one another – seemingly in approval. During this time King goes off, removes tunic and puts on long cloak, completely hiding his clothes.

Narrator   At last it was the day of the Grand Parade. The King went to try on the suit.

King enters, wearing cloak, and goes over to the two tailors.

King   *(Looking at table)* It is so beautiful! I can't wait to try it on!

Narrator   The King couldn't see anything but he did not want to be thought a fool.

The King takes his cloak off, revealing shorts and vest. The tailors pretend to take the suit from the table and help him to put it on. King pretends to be pleased.

Both tailors   You look fantastic, Your Majesty.
It fits beautifully.

Narrator   The Grand Parade begins.

Music. The King and Prime Minister march up and down in the front of the stage.
A crowd gathers, including the tailors. The little boy is at the front.
As the King passes, he shouts.

Boy   The King has got no clothes on!

Narrator   The King realises he has been tricked
and rushes back to grab his cloak.

King does this, puts on cloak and comes to the front again.

King   I have been very silly.
It is not the clothes that matter,
but the person who wears them.
I will be a better King from now on.

31. Let us pray.

PRAYER

This is said by the whole class.

Dear Lord Jesus,
We thank you for the clothes
that keep us warm and dry.
Help us to understand the reasons
why people dress differently.
Help us to understand that
it is how people behave that matters
and not what they are wearing.

                                        Amen

As the children leave the assembly you could play 'The King is in the Altogether',
sung by Danny Kaye.

BACKDROP

A large picture showing nature in spring. The animals can be painted or done in collage by the children.

CHECKLIST

- Backdrop

- Children's seating arrangements

- Record-player

- Record: 'Spring' from *The Four Seasons* by Vivaldi

- Spring flower picture

- Painting of tree in blossom

- Painting of daffodils

- Painting of nesting bird

- Painting of frogspawn and tadpoles

- Painting of spring-cleaning

- Old bird's nest

- Nesting material: twigs, string, wool, paper, mud, moss, straw

- Mime: props – head and wings for bird, table, chairs, stool, doll and cradle, plates, and other items from the home corner

- Bird-table bar-chart

- Seed-growth experiment: seeds on cotton wool; spindly growth; healthy growth

- Picture of sun and cloud

- Large valentine card

- Frying-pan and paper pancake

- Masks

- Bonfire picture

- Paper lanterns or pictures of them

- Painting of Easter eggs

- Puppet play: animals and their homes
    front-board scene
    puppets: two birds, rabbit, hedgehog, bat, fish, fieldmouse
    paintings: pile of leaves, burrow, cave, pond, cornfield, house

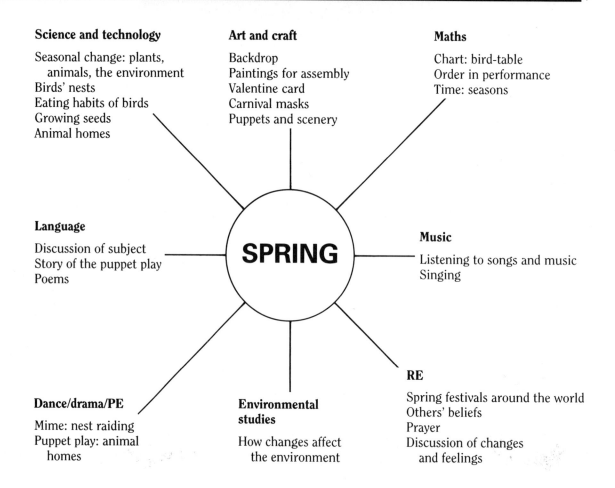

Science and technology

Seasonal change: plants,
　　animals, the environment
Birds' nests
Eating habits of birds
Growing seeds
Animal homes

Art and craft

Backdrop
Paintings for assembly
Valentine card
Carnival masks
Puppets and scenery

Maths

Chart: bird-table
Order in performance
Time: seasons

Language

Discussion of subject
Story of the puppet play
Poems

SPRING

Music

Listening to songs and music
Singing

RE

Spring festivals around the world
Others' beliefs
Prayer
Discussion of changes
　　and feelings

Dance/drama/PE

Mime: nest raiding
Puppet play: animal
　　homes

**Environmental
studies**

How changes affect
　　the environment

THE ASSEMBLY: Spring ▶

For entry into the assembly, play 'Spring' from *The Four Seasons* by Vivaldi.

1. Good morning everybody.
   Welcome to our spring-time assembly.

2. Spring is a season. It is the time when some plants and animals awaken after the coldness of winter.

3. The 21st of March is officially the first day of spring, but we often see signs of spring as early as February.

4. We can see snowdrops and crocuses pushing through the soil.

Child holds up picture.

5. We can see buds on the trees and later we can look for blossom of pink and white and yellow.

Child holds up picture.

6. The days grow longer and the weather becomes a little warmer. Daffodils appear.

Child holds up picture.

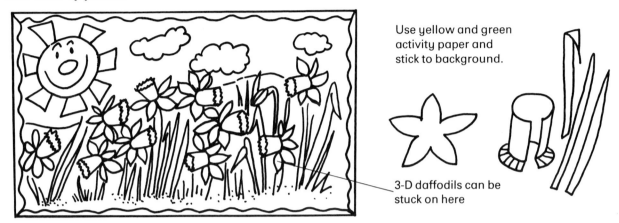

Use yellow and green activity paper and stick to background.

3-D daffodils can be stuck on here

7. Birds return from migration and start to build their nests.

Child holds up picture.

8. We can look for frogspawn in ponds and watch for little tadpoles.

Child holds up picture.

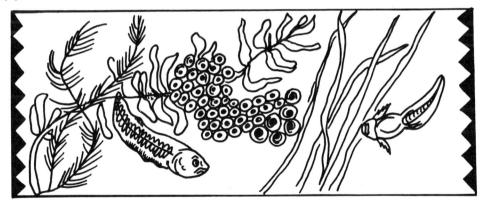

9. In the house we start spring-cleaning and we can see the garden beginning to grow again.

POEMS

The poems overleaf can be read by individuals or by small groups in a chorus.

A Little Bit of Blowing

A little bit of blowing, a little bit of snow,
A little bit of growing and the crocuses will show.
On every twig that's lonely, a new green leaf will spring,
On every patient tree-top a thrush will perch and sing.

What the Leaves Said

The leaves said, "It's spring,
And here are we
Opening and stretching
On every tree."

The leaves said, "It's summer,
Each bird has a nest.
We make the shadow
Where they can rest."

The leaves said, "It's autumn,
Aren't we all gay?"
Scarlet and golden
And russet were they.

The leaves said, "It's winter,
Weary are we."
So they lay down and slept
Under a tree.

I know a Little Pussy

I know a little pussy,
Her coat is silver-grey,
She lives down in the meadow
Not very far away.
Although she is a pussy,
She'll never be a cat,
For she's a pussy-willow . . .
Now what do you think of that?

Spring is just around the corner,
    Birds will try their best,
With twigs and string, all sorts of things,
    To make a cosy nest.

Spring is just around the corner,
    Flowers are coming too,
Waving golden daffodils,
    Crocus white and blue.

Spring is just around the corner,
    Feel the warming sun,
Sweep away those winter days
    Spring-cleaning to be done!

10. A bird is very clever. Using only its beak,
it can make a nest out of mud and twigs
and different materials like wool and paper.

Child holds up a bird's nest abandoned from last year.
Note: This is not essential, and you should in any case supply the nest yourself; do
not encourage the children to look for nests, even abandoned ones. Bird's-nesting of
any sort causes disturbance, and a nest that appears to be abandoned may still be in
use as a shelter for birds, animals and insects.

11. We have collected things to make a nest.
Who would like to try to make a nest?

A child could be invited from the audience.

You can only use one hand. All the things you need
are on that table.

12. Here is a scene for you to watch while *(child's name)*
tries to make a nest.

MIMED PLAY

Props
Table, chairs, stool, plates, doll in cradle and anything else available from the home corner to make a domestic setting.

Characters
Mum,   Dad,   large bird.

Costumes
Everyday clothes for Mum and Dad; cardboard head and wings for bird, worn with appropriately coloured clothes.

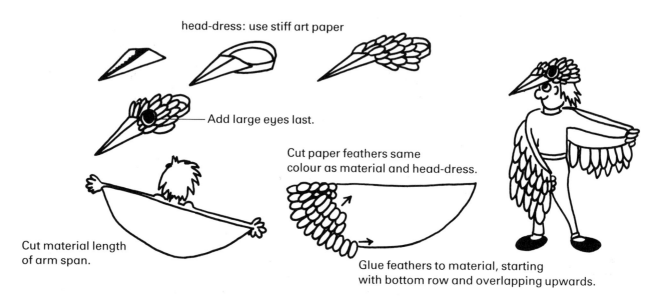

head-dress: use stiff art paper

Add large eyes last.

Cut paper feathers same colour as material and head-dress.

Cut material length of arm span.

Glue feathers to material, starting with bottom row and overlapping upwards.

The children mime the following scene.

Mum and Dad are seated at the table having a meal and chatting. A large bird comes in, turns over the stool and a chair, upsets various other articles, and finally picks up the baby and 'flies' off with it. The parents run away and huddle in a corner when the bird enters. They should look very frightened – shaking, teeth chattering. When the bird has gone they return to their home and look at all the damage. They realise their baby has gone and they begin to cry.

13. How would you feel if a giant creature came into your house and wrecked it?

14. This may be how a bird feels when people raid its nest and steal the eggs.

15. We should protect birds and guard their nests and their eggs and the places where they live.

16. We made a bird table and put lots of different foods on it to see which foods the birds liked most of all.

Child holds up bar-chart, or points to chart on display. (Of course, the information will need to be gathered in the weeks preceding the assembly.)

This artwork is just an example of the recording; older children could write in each space.

17. *(To child who has been building the nest)*
Stop building now. We can see how hard it is
to make a nest, so we should not disturb birds at all.

18. We planted some seeds in our classroom.
We kept some in the dark, with no water.
Nothing happened.

Child holds up tray of seeds on dry paper towelling or cotton wool.

19. We watered some and kept them in the dark.
They grew thin and weak with no colour.

Child holds up tray with seedlings like this.

20. We watered some and placed them on a sunny window-sill. These grew best of all, strong, tall and green.

Child holds up tray with healthy seedlings.

21. Plants need heat, light and water to grow well. That is why plants begin to grow in the spring, when it is warmer, wet and sunny.

Child holds up painting of sun and rain-cloud.

SONG

At this stage the class could sing 'All the Flowers are Waking' from *Someone's Singing, Lord* published by A. & C. Black.

22. There are many festivals and celebrations in spring. One of the first is St Valentine's Day on 14th February.

Child holds up giant valentine card and recites.

Roses are red, violets are blue,
Sugar is sweet and so are you.

23. On Shrove Tuesday we have pancakes for tea. We can toss them in a pan.

Child tosses 'pancake' made of several yellow paper discs glued together.

24. Carnivals take place in many countries in spring. In France, the carnival is called Mardi Gras.

Children hold masks over their faces.

Cut from card and decorate with sequins, glitter and felt pens.

Add crepe paper feathers.

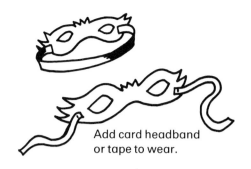

Add card headband or tape to wear.

25. The Hindu festival of Holi celebrates the arrival of spring. It is also a fire festival and bonfires are lit.

Child holds up picture of a bonfire.

26. Sikhs have a similar festival called Hola or Hola Mohalla.

27. The Chinese have a lantern festival and Ching Ming, the festival of pure brightness.

Child holds up a paper lantern or a painting of one.

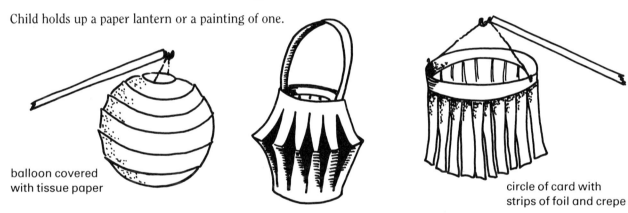

balloon covered with tissue paper

circle of card with strips of foil and crepe

28. All these festivals celebrate the arrival of spring.

29. We celebrate Easter at this time of the year and we look forward to receiving chocolate eggs.

Child holds up picture of eggs.

30. Jewish families celebrate Pesach or the Passover. They eat a special meal called the Seder.

31. Lots of things happen in the spring. It is a busy time of year.

PUPPET PLAY

A puppet play could be included here. It is performed from behind an upright board on which a spring-time country scene is displayed. The board should be high enough for children just to reach the top. Make sure the board is secure because young children tend to press forward when performing with puppets.

These are the characters.

Two birds cut from card and slotted into garden sticks or canes.

A rabbit made from an old sock, with cardboard ears.

A hedgehog made from an old sock, with fringed material sewn on to represent prickles.

A bat cut from card, folded down the middle and slotted into a stick or cane.

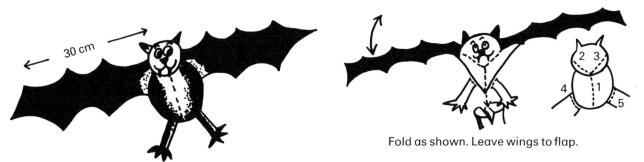

30 cm

2 3
4 1
5

Fold as shown. Leave wings to flap.

A fish cut from cardboard, decorated both sides and stuck into a split stick or cane.

A fieldmouse made from an old sock, with felt ears, button nose and eyes, string whiskers and a woollen tail.

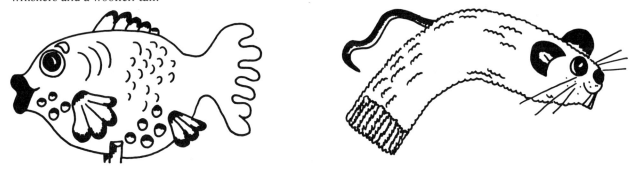

These are the pictures that are needed. Mount them on card cut-outs.

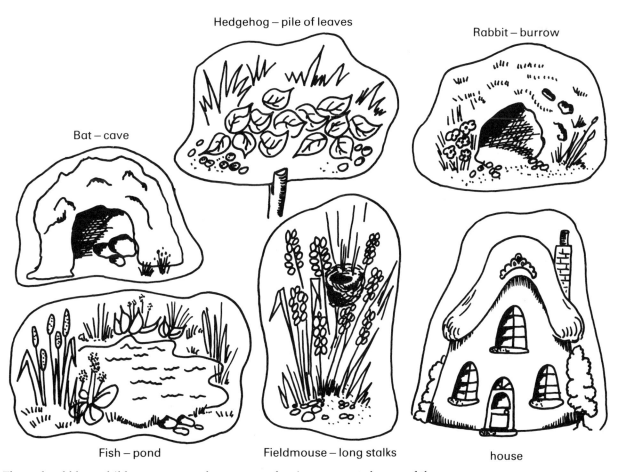

Hedgehog – pile of leaves

Rabbit – burrow

Bat – cave

Fish – pond

Fieldmouse – long stalks

house

There should be a child to operate each puppet so that it appears at the top of the board at the appropriate time. The teacher acts as narrator, or other children take turns.

Narrator 1	Two birds had returned from migration and they were looking for a place to build a nest.
Both birds	Oh, I don't think we'll ever find a good place.
Hedgehog	Why don't you come and look at my nest? I like it very much and I'm sure you will too.

Child holds up picture of hedgehog's nest and they go over to it.

Birds	It is a beautiful nest, but it's not quite right. Our eggs might get broken on the floor like that.
Narrator 2	Hedgehog leaves and Rabbit comes along.
Rabbit	Why don't you come and look at my hole? I like it very much and I'm sure you will too.

Child holds up picture of rabbit's burrow and they go over to it.

Birds	It is a beautiful hole, but it's not quite right. It's too deep underground.
Narrator 3	Rabbit goes away and Bat appears.
Bat	Why don't you come and look at my cave?

Child holds up picture of bat's cave and they go over to it.

Birds	It is a beautiful cave, but it's not quite right. It's too dark.
Narrator 4	Bat goes away and a fish calls from its pond.

Fish   Why don't you come into my pond?

Child holds up picture of fish-pond and they go over to it.

Birds   It is a beautiful pond, but it's not quite right. It's too wet.

Narrator 5   The fish goes away and Fieldmouse appears.

Fieldmouse   Why don't you come and look at my nest in the long grass?

Child holds up picture of fieldmouse's nest and they go over to it.

Birds   It is a beautiful nest, but it's not quite right. It's too small.

One bird   Isn't that where we built our nest last year, just under the roof of that house?

Child holds up picture of house and they go over to it.

Second bird   It's just right!
We have found the perfect place
to build our nest.

PRAYER

The prayer can be read by one child, or by the class in chorus.

Dear Lord Jesus,
Thank you for the new life and growth of spring.
Help us to look after all God's creatures
and to care for living things.
Thank you for sunshine and rain,
for the flowers and the birds,
and the sea and the sky.   Amen

To end the assembly the school could sing 'Feed the Birds' from *Mary Poppins*, or
you could play the music or the record.

FOOD

BACKDROP

Our favourite foods!

children's own
paintings of food

Paint and cut out chef. Add crepe paper base and canopy.

CHECKLIST

- Backdrop

- Children's seating arrangements

- Record-player

- Record: 'Food, Glorious Food' from the musical *Oliver*

- Painting of breakfast food

- Painting of lunch/dinner

- Painting of supper

- Painting of drinks

- Painting of fizzy drinks (or collage of advertisements)

- Painting of hot-dogs

- Painting of toad-in-the-hole

- Painting of bubble and squeak

- Painting of bangers and mash

- Pictures and posters of favourite lollies and ice-creams

- Bowl of apples, carrots and celery

- Bowl of oranges, grapefruit and blackcurrants

- Picture/painting of Christmas food

- Painting of treacle toffee and parkin

- Painting of pancakes

- Painting of hot-cross buns

- Painting of Easter eggs

- Play: *The Enormous Turnip*
    backdrop: painting of a farmhouse in the country
    props: large painting of a turnip (big enough to conceal a child)
    costumes: peasant clothes for six children, i.e. trousers, shirts, waistcoats, cloth caps and boots/wellies for the men; long or calf-length skirts, aprons, blouses, shawls, headscarves for the women

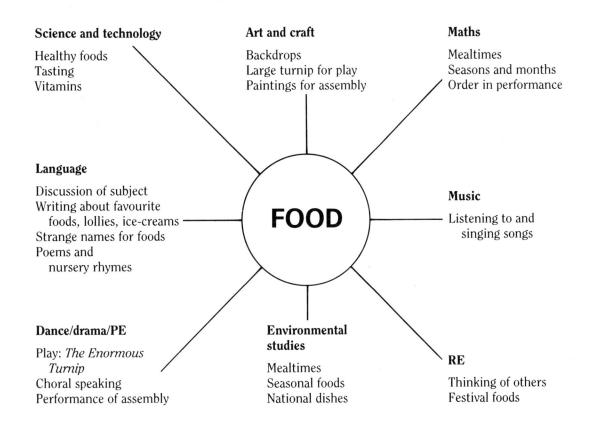

Science and technology

Healthy foods
Tasting
Vitamins

Art and craft

Backdrops
Large turnip for play
Paintings for assembly

Maths

Mealtimes
Seasons and months
Order in performance

Language

Discussion of subject
Writing about favourite
    foods, lollies, ice-creams
Strange names for foods
Poems and
    nursery rhymes

FOOD

Music

Listening to and
    singing songs

Dance/drama/PE

Play: *The Enormous
    Turnip*
Choral speaking
Performance of assembly

**Environmental
studies**

Mealtimes
Seasonal foods
National dishes

RE

Thinking of others
Festival foods

THE ASSEMBLY: Food ▶

MUSIC

For entry into the assembly, play 'Food, Glorious Food' from the musical *Oliver* by
Lionel Bart.

1. Good morning everybody. Welcome to our assembly.
   It's all about food.

2. Food is everything we eat. It keeps us alive.
   We eat food at certain times in the day.

3. The times are called breakfast, lunch, tea,
   dinner, supper.

4. We start the day with breakfast.
   We usually eat some of these things.

Child holds up picture of breakfast foods.

5. Dinner is the main meal of the day.
   We usually have dinner in the middle of the day.
   This midday meal is sometimes called lunch.

Meat, potatoes and peas

Beefburger and chips

Apple pie and custard

Salad

Ice-cream

6. Some people have dinner at night. They might eat some of these things. Lots of people call this meal tea.

Child holds up picture of dinner/tea foods.

7. Supper is the meal we have before we go to bed. Usually it is a very light meal.

Child holds up picture of supper foods.

Baked beans on toast

Sandwiches

Milk and biscuits

8. Dear God,
   We thank you that we can choose between so many good things to eat. Help us to remember those who are not so lucky, and those who sometimes do not have any food at all. Help us to share our gifts so that everyone can have enough food to eat.

   Amen

9. We need to drink as well as eat.
   We would die if we didn't drink.

10. There are lots of different things for us to drink.
    Water. Milk. Tea. Coffee. Wine. Squash.

    Child holds up picture of these drinks and points to each as he or she says the name.

11. Lots of children like fizzy drinks like this.

    Child holds up picture of cola, lemonade, orangeade, etc.

12. Some foods have strange names.
    A sausage in a bread bun is called a hot-dog.

    Child holds up picture.

13. Sausages cooked in batter is called toad-in-the-hole.

    Child holds up a picture.

14. A mixture of vegetables fried in a pan is called bubble and squeak.

    Child holds up a picture.

15. Sausages and mashed potato is called bangers and mash.

16. Certain foods are linked with certain countries.
    Here are some.
    England and roast beef.
    France and snails or frogs' legs.
    Scotland and haggis.
    Italy and spaghetti.

17. India and curry.
    America and hamburgers.
    Germany and sausages.
    China and rice.

18. Lots of people like lollies and ice-cream.

Before the assembly, let the children paint pictures and write about their favourite lollies and ice-creams. Two or three of them hold up their illustrations at this stage, and read what they have written.

19. Fruit and vegetables are very good for our teeth
    and digestion. Apples, carrots and celery are
    very good for our teeth.

Child holds up picture.

20. Oranges, blackcurrants and grapefruit are
    full of vitamin C. Vitamins and fibre keep us healthy.

21. Here are some poems about food.

POEMS

These can be arranged for choral speaking, or read by individual children. Choose about four poems.

Brown potatoes, white potatoes,
Change them if you can,
Turn them into golden chips
Frying in the pan.

Porridge is bubbling, bubbling hot,
Stir it round and round in the pot.
The bubbles plip and the bubbles plop.
It's ready to eat, all bubbling hot.

Food

Shrove Tuesday, Ash Wednesday,
When Jack went to plough,
His mother made pancakes;
She didn't know how.
She tossed them, she turned them,
She burned them quite black;
She put in some pepper and
Poisoned poor Jack.

Peas

I always eat peas with honey,
I've done it all my life,
They do taste kind of funny
But it keeps them on the knife.

I wish I was a little grub
With whiskers round my tummy.
I'd climb into a honey pot
And make my tummy gummy.

The man in the moon came down too soon
    And asked his way to Norwich.
He went by the south and burnt his mouth
    With eating cold plum porridge.

Hens

Hicketey Picketey my black hen,
She lays eggs for gentlemen,
Sometimes nine and sometimes ten,
Hicketey Picketey my black hen.

There was a young lady from Lymm
Who was so excessively thin
That when she essayed
To drink lemonade
She slipped through the straw and fell in.

As well as the poems, you could use any of these nursery rhymes: 'Little Miss Muffet'; 'Tom, Tom, the Piper's Son'; 'Little Tommy Tucker'; 'Jack Spratt'; 'The Knave of Hearts'; 'Simple Simon'.

22. We often have special food on special days. At Christmas we have turkey and plum pudding and mince pies.

Child holds up a picture.

23. On bonfire night we have treacle toffee and sticky cake called parkin.

24. On Shrove Tuesday we have pancakes.

Child holds up a picture.

25. On Good Friday we eat hot-cross buns

(child holds up picture)

and we sing *(class sings the following song)*:

Hot-cross buns, hot-cross buns,
One a penny, two a penny,
Hot-cross buns.
If you have no daughters
Give them to your sons.
One a penny, two a penny,
Hot-cross buns.

26. On Easter Sunday we give Easter eggs made of chocolate.

Child holds up picture.

**27. Our play is about food.
It is the story of an enormous turnip.**

PLAY

The Enormous Turnip

Backdrop
A large painting of a farmhouse in the country.

Props
A large painting of a turnip (big enough to conceal a child). For a 3-D effect, paint two sides of the turnip and staple or sew them together as shown, leaving arm/hand holes.

Characters
Farmer, farmer's wife, their son, their daughter, grandfather, grandmother, the enormous turnip, narrator.

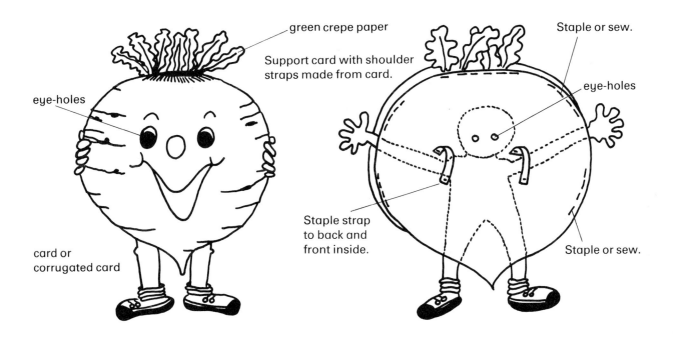

Costumes
Peasant clothes: trousers, shirts, waistcoats, cloth caps and boots/wellies for the men; long or calf-length skirts, aprons, blouses, shawls and headscarves for the women.

The story begins with the farmer's wife in the farmyard, looking at the enormous turnip.

Wife   I think that turnip is quite big enough. We shall have turnip soup tonight.

Narrator   She bent down and pulled and pulled but the turnip would not move.

Wife mimes pulling and tugging.

Wife   I shall need some help. Husband, come and help me pull up the turnip and we shall have soup for tea.

Narrator   The farmer came and he pulled with his wife, but the turnip would not move.

Farmer enters during narrator's speech and mimes tugging with his wife.

Farmer   We shall need some help. Children, come and help us pull up the turnip and we shall have soup for tea.

Narrator   The farmer's children came and pulled with their parents, but the turnip would not move.

Son and daughter enter during narrator's speech and mime tugging with their parents.

Farmer, wife and children   We need more help. Grandfather, Grandmother, come and help us pull up the turnip and we shall have soup for tea.

Narrator   The grandparents came and they pulled with everyone else. They pulled and they pulled and at last the turnip came up. They all rolled over.

Grandparents enter during narrator's speech and mime tugging with the rest of the family. Suddenly, the turnip runs towards them (keeping face to audience). The family staggers backwards.

Wife   Now we can all have some turnip soup for tea.

Narrator   The farmer's wife cooked the turnip and it was delicious. This story helps us to remember that if we help each other and work together, we can overcome even very difficult problems.

SONGS

To end the assembly, the class or the whole school could sing one of these songs, and the tune of another could be played as the school leaves the hall:

'Food, Glorious Food', from the musical *Oliver*; 'Tea for Two'; 'Boiled Beef and Carrots'; 'Oranges and Lemons'.

PEOPLE WHO HELP US

BACKDROP

Position sticky-tape on jigsaw pieces before the assembly starts.

Cut the jigsaw pieces from large sheets of activity paper and mount the figures on them. The backing is corrugated card, smooth side uppermost. The central picture of the child and the various pictures of the teachers can be in position prior to the assembly. The children merely add the teachers' names at the appropriate time. The other figures – cook, caretaker, etc – are positioned after the assembly, to consolidate the idea of all the members of the community co-operating.

CHECKLIST ▶

- Backdrop

- Children's seating arrangements

- Record-player

- Records: 'From Me to You', 'I'll Get By with a little Help from my Friends', 'A Hard Day's Night' and 'Help!', all by The Beatles; 'He's got the Whole World in His Hands', which is available on many folk records

- Painting of house

- People in school: either seven paintings with holes for faces, or costumes for the seven people depicted

- Name cards for teachers

- Portraits of teachers (already mounted on backdrop)

- List of the names of parent helpers

- Children's own writing about their friends

- Policeman's and/or policewoman's uniform

- Doctor's coat and 'stethoscope'

- Nurse's uniform

- Shopkeeper's clothes

- Play: *Neighbours*
  props/costumes: chair, blanket, shopping bag, headscarf, baby's bonnet and dummy, old lady's hat

- Puppet play: *The Monkey and the Jar of Water*
  props: table, green crepe paper, painting of jungle, transparent plastic jug half full of water, stones, glove-puppet monkey or large toy monkey, toy snake or door-stop/stuffed sock

TOPIC WEB ▶

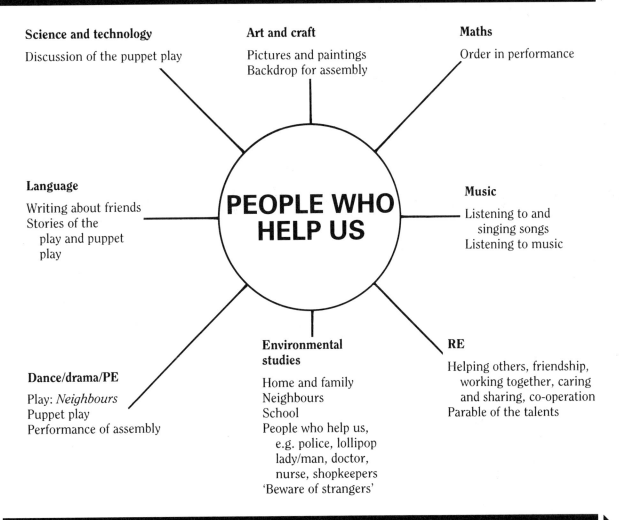

Science and technology
Discussion of the puppet play

Art and craft
Pictures and paintings
Backdrop for assembly

Maths
Order in performance

Language
Writing about friends
Stories of the
   play and puppet
   play

PEOPLE WHO HELP US

Music
Listening to and
   singing songs
Listening to music

Dance/drama/PE
Play: *Neighbours*
Puppet play
Performance of assembly

Environmental studies
Home and family
Neighbours
School
People who help us,
   e.g. police, lollipop
   lady/man, doctor,
   nurse, shopkeepers
'Beware of strangers'

RE
Helping others, friendship,
   working together, caring
   and sharing, co-operation
Parable of the talents

THE ASSEMBLY: People who help us ▶

MUSIC

For entry into the assembly, play 'From me to you' or 'I'll Get By with a little Help from my Friends', both by The Beatles; or 'He's got the Whole World in His Hands', which is available on several folk records.

1. Good morning everybody.
   Our assembly is about people who help us.

2. We've been talking and we've discovered that there are lots of people who help us every day, and quite a few who need us to help them.

3. We need a great deal of help because we are children and we are learning about life.

4. Our parents love and care for us every day.
   They give us a home and food and clothes and toys
   . . . and a good telling off sometimes!
   Everyone in a family cares for each other.

   Child holds up picture of a house/block of flats.

5. Our parents need our help with little jobs like keeping our rooms tidy.

6. Our teachers care for us and help us to learn new and exciting things each day.

7. They teach us how to live together in a big group like a class *(indicates class with arm)* or a school *(indicates the audience)*.

8. There are many people who help us at school. Everyone works together.

   For the next section, about people in school, the children can paint large pictures of the individuals concerned, and cut out each face, leaving a hole as in seaside photos, so that the speaker can show his or her own face. For display later on, simply stick paper on the back over each hole and paint in the face. Alternatively, the children can dress up as the people, using items from the home corner and perhaps things borrowed from the subject, e.g. a recognisable necklace or apron or headscarf. All the children involved remain standing until this section is finished.

9. I'm *(name)*, the cook, who tries to make delicious meals each day. Today's dinner is *(name of meal)*.

10. I'm *(name)*, one of the helpers in the kitchen who helps cook. The other helpers are *(names)*.

11. I'm *(name)*, one of the welfare assistants who look after you all at dinner time and playtime. The other assistants are *(names)*. We do have some fun together, don't we?

12. I'm *(name)*, the nursery nurse, and I help you in the classroom, with your teacher.

13. I'm *(name)*, the school secretary, who works in the school office, typing, answering the phone and doing lots of other jobs.

14. I'm *(name)*, the school caretaker, who keeps the school clean and tidy.

15. I'm *(name)*, one of the cleaners who help *(caretaker's name)*. The other cleaners are *(names)*.

All seven children sit.

For the next section, about the teachers, the paintings can be ready-mounted on the backdrop and the children who say the names can each hold the corresponding name label. When a child's turn comes, he or she sticks the name under the appropriate picture. Fix loops of sticky tape on the back of each label, and sit the children near the backdrop. (The pictures of the other seven 'workers' can be added to the display later on, when it becomes a more permanent exhibit.)

16. Here are the teachers in our school.

Several children take turns to say a name and fix a label.

17. Some parents also come in to help us.

Child holds up list of names, if not too long.

18. Already you can see just how many people help us each day at school. We need every one of them, because they all do different jobs to keep our school going.

19. I think we've forgotten some.

20. Oh, who are they?

19. Our friends in school.

20. Oh yes of course.
    If you are real friends, you help each other.

21. Some of us have written about how our friends help us.

    Prior to the assembly, ask the children to write a short piece each about a friend.
    Invite three of the children to read out their work, each standing near the friend so
    that the child can put a hand on the friend's shoulder at the start of the reading.

22. There are other people who help us. They are not
    in our families or part of our school, but they are
    part of our community.

    Child dressed as policeman or policewoman: blue/white shirt, black trousers or skirt,
    tie and hat. You may be able to borrow a hat, or use a toy one. If a representative of
    the police visits your school regularly, insert his or her name in the text.

23. Hello. I'm PC *(name)* and I come into school
    to talk about road safety.
    I hope you all remember the Green Cross Code.
    Let's say it together now.

    The whole class says the code:

    When you want to cross the road, find a safe place
    to cross and stop near the kerb.
    Look all around and listen.
    If there is nothing coming, walk straight across
    the road, still looking and listening.

24. Policemen and women can tell us which way to go
    if we are stuck, and they can help us if we are lost.

25. There are some people who don't want to help children.
    They pretend to help, but they really want to hurt us.
    Who are they?

The whole class responds:

STRANGERS.

26. What do we say to strangers who pretend to help?

The whole class says:

NO!

27. Hello. I'm Doctor *(name)*. You see me at the clinic. This is Nurse *(name)* who comes into school.

Child is dressed in white coat (an old shirt/blouse) and has a stethoscope (black tubing/rope with a weight).

28. We check to see if you are healthy and we can help you if you are sick

Child wears a nurse's uniform.

29. Hello. I'm *(name)*. I work in a shop near your school. I serve you when you come in.

If possible, let child wear things that can be associated with a local shop-keeper, e.g. beard, glasses, beads, brown coat, sari.

30. We also have neighbours. These are people who live near us.

You could play the theme from the TV programme *Neighbours*, while the children prepare for the drama.

PLAY

Neighbours

Props/costumes
Chair with blanket over it, shopping bag, old lady's hat, headscarf, baby's bonnet and dummy.

Characters
Mrs Brown (an old lady), Mrs Watson (a young woman), a baby,
Mr Hall (the baby's dad).

Mrs Brown is sitting in the chair, legs wrapped in the blanket. There is the sound of a knock at the door.

Mrs Brown	Hello? Come in. The door's open.
Mrs Watson	Morning, Mrs Brown. How are you today?
Mrs Brown	Oh, not so bad, love. But my legs are a bit wobbly, you know. Would you get me a small loaf if you go down to the shops?
Mrs Watson	You know I always do. Brown for Mrs Brown?
Mrs Brown	Yes, I eat brown and I am Brown, hee hee. Has that new family moved into number 36 yet?
Mrs Watson	Yes, the removal van has just arrived and Mrs Hall, next to me, is making them all a cup of tea. They all look worn out.

Mr Hall enters with the baby. Baby crawling.

Baby	Goo ga dee dee goo goo. (*etc.*)
Mr Hall	Morning, Mrs Brown dear. Are you feeling good?
Mrs Brown	Yes, love.
Mr Hall	Jean, my wife, is doing her good neighbour bit and helping that new family to move in. I'm going to help lift the cooker. *(To Mrs Watson)* If you are going to the park, would you take our "terror"?

Mrs Watson	'Course I will. He's a little darling, a little cracker!
Baby	*(Looking pleased)* Goo goo.
Mrs Brown	Ay, I don't know what any of us would do without our neighbours.
Mr Hall	We've all got to lend a hand.

SONG

The whole class sings a song about friendship, for example 'Magic Penny', from *Alleluya*, published by A. & C. Black; or 'Stick on a Smile', from *Every Colour Under the Sun*, published by Ward Lock Educational.

31. Of course we mustn't forget to help ourselves
by trying hard with everything we do.
Helping ourselves is part of growing up.

32. Here is a story about a little monkey who tried
very hard. He thought for himself and had a go.

PUPPET PLAY

The Monkey and the Jar of Water

Props
Small table covered with green crepe paper or a painting of a jungle; very large transparent plastic jug half full of water; pile of large stones.

Characters
Monkey (a glove puppet or toy furry monkey – as large as possible) is operated by one child.
Snake (a toy snake, furry door-stop or stuffed sock) is operated by a second child.
Narrator.

Note: The children working the puppets need not be out of sight, but can stand behind the table and move the toys in mime. When Monkey puts the stones in the jug, the child does this and simply moves the toy to mask his or her hand.

green crepe frill
to cover join

Narrator   It was a hot day in the jungle and Monkey and Snake lay in the long grass, feeling thirsty.

Monkey   I'm so thirsty. I'd love a long cool drink.

Snake   So would I, but it's such a long way to the river. And we would never reach the water in that jar. *(Points to jar.)*

Monkey   There's water in there?
Why didn't you say so?

Narrator   Monkey went to the jar and looked over the edge, deep down to the water. He tried to stretch his arm down to it, but it was too far.

Snake	Knock it over, then we can drink it when it spills. I can't be bothered to wait longer.
Monkey	That's silly. It would soak into the dry ground and we would get very little.
Narrator	Monkey sat and thought for a minute and looked around him. *(Monkey does this.)* He saw some stones on the ground and had an idea. He picked them up one by one and dropped them into the pot.

Child puts stones into the jug . . . gently!

Narrator	As he put in each stone, the water rose, until at last it was near the top and he could sip it easily.
Monkey	*(Sipping)* Delicious cool water! Come and get some, Snake.
Snake	It's too much trouble to climb up there.
Narrator	So Snake stayed thirsty and Monkey, who used his brain and helped himself, was refreshed.

33. There's another good story of a man who helped himself and made the best use of his talents. It's called *The Parable of the Talents* and it is a story that Jesus told. Ask your teacher to tell it to you.

PRARYER

34. Dear God,
As we grow up, help us to think about others and
to do what we can to help them. Guide us each day
to think a little more for ourselves.
For all the people who love and care for us,
we thank you Father.

Amen

35. We hope you will think about what we have shared
with you in our assembly. Please sing this song with us.

SONG

Choose a song from this selection:

'Think, think on these Things', or 'When I needed a Neighbour', or 'If I had a Hammer', all from *Someone's Singing, Lord*, published by A. & C. Black.

'Do your best' or 'We will take care of you' from *Every Colour Under the Sun*, published by Ward Lock Educational.

At the end of the assembly, the school could leave the hall to either 'A Hard Day's Night' or 'Help!', both by The Beatles.

CONSIDERATION

BACKDROP

Fix picture to corrugated card. Use rounders posts for support in the roll at each end.

A backdrop of your playground can be used as the setting for the modern-day version of the story of The Good Samaritan. Later this can be the base for a classroom display, with pictures of the characters in the play surrounded by the children's writing about consideration.

CHECKLIST ▶

- Backdrop

- Children's seating arrangements

- Painting of *Goldilocks and the Three Bears*

- Painting of Baby Bear (upset)

- Painting of Cinderella

- Cup and saucer on tray

- Postman's or postwoman's hat and bag

- Letter in envelope

- Play: *The Good Samaritan*
    props: picture (for Martin)
    costumes: Sikh clothes (including turban) for one boy. Alternatively, clothes for a boy belonging to any other group for whom a particular hat/headgear is daily wear (adapt script accordingly). The other children wear their everyday clothes, but Martin must have a hat/cap.

- Charity poster or poster of Bob Geldof

- Scroll for the 'School roll of honour'

- Paintings of six people on this roll

- A bag of sweets and a toy

- Small wrapped present

- Play: *The Guardian*
  props: large cardboard box covered on four sides with 'wall' motif; short tape of Superman music; tape-recorder; felt-tipped pens
  costumes: The Guardian's 'Superman' outfit (large letter G on chest)

TOPIC WEB ▶

Language

Stories: *Goldilocks and the Three Bears*, *Cinderella*, *The Good Samaritan*, *The Guardian*
Children's own writing

Art and craft

Backdrop
Paintings for assembly
Scroll of honour

Maths

Order in performance

CONSIDERATION

Music

Listening to and singing songs

Drama/dance/PE

Mime: rude behaviour
Play: *The Good Samaritan*
Play: *The Guardian*
Performance of assembly

Environmental studies

Charity work
Helping at home/school
Sharing
Caring for the environment

RE

What it means to be considerate/inconsiderate
The story of *The Good Samaritan*
Charity work
Helping and sharing

THE ASSEMBLY: Consideration ▶

1. *(Teacher)* Good morning everybody.
   Today we want you to think very hard about things you will see and hear in our assembly.

2. We are going to tell you about something called consideration. Do you know what that is . . . apart from being a very long word?

3. If you are a considerate person you think about other people and how you can help them.
In a way, it means being kind and thoughtful.

4. Do you know the story of *Goldilocks and the Three Bears?* Goldilocks just walked into their house and used their things without asking.

Child holds up picture of the characters in the story.

5. Baby Bear was upset when he found his porridge eaten, his chair broken and his bed slept in.

Child holds up picture of upset baby bear.

6. Goldilocks just thought about herself.
She wasn't considerate; she was very inconsiderate.

7. Do you know the story of *Cinderella*?

Child holds up picture of Cinderella.

Well, the Ugly Sisters . . .

Child is interrupted by three children who burst into the hall noisily and bang the door. They should enter by the door nearest to the front of the stage, pretending to be late for assembly. They push and jostle their class mates, chatter and knock over chairs, and eventually make their way to the front, where they stand giggling.

7. *(Continues)* . . . as I was saying, the Ugly Sisters weren't considerate at all. They didn't care if Cinderella was left at home, sad and lonely, while they enjoyed themselves, but . . .

The three at the front begin to argue noisily:

8. This is boring. Let's sit down.

9. No, stay here. We'll get the best view.

10. It's a daft story anyway.

11. *(Teacher)* Excuse me, but you three children were very late and you just burst in without any thought for the people who were trying to listen to the story.

The three children look very surprised. The teacher turns to the rest of the class and says:

Do any of you know what they should have done?

12. They should have come in quietly.

13. *(Teacher)* Yes, that would have been more considerate. *(Teacher turns to the three in the front.)* Now please try to sit quietly. What *(child no. 7's name)* was going to say was that, in the end, Cinderella was much kinder than her sisters because she forgave them and they went to live in the palace. *(Sits)* Oh, I'm worn out now, with all the excitement.

14. Here Mrs/Mr/Miss *(teacher's name)*, you look very tired. You look as though you could do with a cup of tea.

Child goes over to teacher, carrying a small tray holding a plastic cup and saucer.

15. *(Teacher)* Oh, thanks . . . how considerate of you.

Pretends to drink tea and visibly relax.

16. Child dressed as postman/postwoman and carrying a satchel goes up to and speaks to the teacher.

Excuse me Mrs/Mr/Miss *(teacher's name)*, may I give this letter to *(name of speaker 17)*?

Teacher nods. Child goes over to speaker 17, takes an envelope from the satchel and hands it to speaker 17.

Here's an urgent letter – first class.

17. Thanks.

Child opens envelope, takes out letter and pretends to read.

Oh, it's from Mrs Tompson. Oh, dear . . .
(Reads letter aloud): Dear *(name of speaker 17)*,
I do hope that there is nothing wrong with you.
I thought that you were poorly or that you had had
an accident when you didn't turn up yesterday.
I was rather worried, but then my neighbour saw you
at the park. I had made your favourite cake
and chocolate fingers for tea. Please let me know
if everything is all right.
Your friend Mrs Tompson.

Oh, no! I forgot I was expected for tea and I went
to the park. How inconsiderate of me.
I must go round and say I'm sorry.

18. Jesus used to tell a story about someone who showed
a great deal of consideration to a complete stranger.
It is the story of The Good Samaritan.

19. This is how the story might look in our playground
today.

PLAY

The Good Samaritan

Backdrop
Use the assembly backdrop, depicting your playground.

Props
A painting for Martin.

Characters

Little Martin (the traveller), Sam (the Samaritan), Fred, Ben, Jenny, Sita (four children), a boy, four rough boys (the robbers), teacher (the innkeeper).

Costumes

Sikh clothes, including turban, for Sam. Alternatively, you can dress Sam in the clothes for a boy belonging to any other group for whom a particular hat/headgear is daily wear (adapt script accordingly). The other children wear everyday clothes, but Martin must have a hat/cap.

All the children except Martin are playing in the playground.

Fred   Oy, you! *(Shouting at Sam)* Why do you wear that funny hat?

Sam   It's not a hat, it's a turban.
All Sikhs wear them because it's part of our religion.

Fred   You look funny!

Sam   So do you!

Fred   You should go to another school.

Sam   I like this one.

Ben   *(To Fred)* Leave Sam alone, he's OK.

Fred   All foreigners are funny, especially Sam.

Ben   Come on dafty!

All three boys exit right.

Jenny   All boys are daft. They play messy games.

Sita   Yes, and they're rough.

Jenny   Come on, let's go in.
I don't want to spoil my clothes.

Girls exit right. Martin enters from the left, carrying picture.

Martin   Oh great, it's school today! I can show
my picture to *(name of headteacher)*.

The four rough boys enter left, after Martin. They knock Martin over, rip his picture, pinch his cap and run offstage, laughing.

Martin   Oh, no. They've spoilt my picture and
I've hurt my leg. I'll be late as well.
(Starts to cry.)

Sita and Jenny enter left. They see Martin but do not approach him.

Sita   Blow! There's a little boy crying.
Hurry up, we don't want to get
our dresses messed up, helping him.

Jenny   He's dreadfully yucky.
Cross over to the other side
and hurry on.

Girls cross stage rapidly and exit right.

Martin   *(Still on floor, holding leg and very upset)*
I wish someone would help me.

A boy enters left. He does not notice Martin at all.

Boy   Oh dear, what time is it? I'll be late.

Boy exits right, in a hurry. Fred and Ben enter left. Ben stops to help, but Fred pulls him away.

Fred   Come on. We've no time for babies.

Fred and Ben exit right. Sam enters left, sees Martin and goes up to him.

Sam   Hello. What's up?

Martin   Some big lads knocked me over.
(He starts to cry again.)
They spoilt my picture *(sob)* and I might
even miss *(teacher's name)'s* assembly.

Sam   Are you hurt?

Martin   Only my knee.

Sam   Here, blow your nose and I'll take you
into school.

*Sam picks Martin up, brushes him down and, holding his hand, takes him into
school – stage right. The teacher comes out to meet them.*

Sam   Here's a little boy.
He's been in a bit of bother.
I found him on the school path.
(To Martin) Bye. You'll be OK now.

Teacher   Thank you! *(Sam exits right.)*
Well, Martin?

Martin   Big boys bashed me up and he helped me.
Lots of others walked past me.

Teacher   Well, how kind.
What a considerate boy he is.
Come on in with me
and I'll make it better.

Martin and teacher exit right.

20. We decided there are lots of kind and considerate people in this school, like . . .

Talk to the class before the assembly and compile a list of about six people you all
think are especially kind and considerate. Give short examples of their kindness.
Pictures can be included too. Speaker 20 can read the list 'of honour', perhaps
written on a large scroll; or individual children can read out the pieces.

PRAYER

1. Hands together, eyes closed.
   May we always try to discover how other people feel
   and come to know when they are feeling sad or lonely.
   We ask you, God, that whatever we do may help
   to bring joy into someone's life.

   Amen

2. A little consideration helps to make the world
   a better place. Bob Geldof thought about
   the starving people in the world, and he helped
   to raise millions of pounds for them.

   Child holds up a charity poster or poster of Bob Geldof.

3. You were very kind and considerate when you
   collected money for . . .

   Child gives details of recent collection for charity.

4. You can be considerate at home by helping
   Mum and Dad to keep the house tidy.
   I'm going to try to be very good.

5. Think about all the hard work *(caretaker's name)*
   and the cleaners do.
   Help to keep the school clean and tidy yourself.

6. Think about how hard the teachers work
   to make school interesting and exciting.
   Help them by behaving well.

7. When we share our sweets and toys with
   someone who hasn't got as much as us,
   we are being considerate.

   Child holds out bag of sweets and toy to his or her neighbour.

28. If some children are alone and sad in the playground, why not ask them to join in your game.
That would be kind and thoughtful.

29. When you are going to give someone a present, think very hard to find something they would really like, even if it is very small.

Child hands his or her neighbour a small present.

30. Oh no, it's those two!

Gaz and Dave, two fun-loving types, enter and the play begins.

PLAY

The *(name of school/community)* Guardian

Backdrop
Use the assembly backdrop, depicting your playground.

Props
A large cardboard box, covered on four sides with 'wall' motif; a short tape of Superman music; tape-recorder; felt-tipped pens.

covered with grey paper and wall lines drawn on sides

Characters
Gaz,   Dave,   The Guardian.

Costumes
Gaz and Dave wear ordinary clothes. The Guardian wears a Superman outfit with a large G on his or her chest.

The wall should be put on the stage quietly as Gaz and Dave enter. The Guardian should be hiding somewhere on stage: surprise is vital!

Dave   I'm fed up, especially of assemblies.

Gaz   Let's have some fun.

Dave   I've got some new felt pens.
Let's try them out.

Gaz	Where?
Dave	Here's a wall. Come on.
Gaz	Won't we get into trouble?
Dave	So what? No one's looking.
Gaz	OK.

They begin to scrawl on the wall.

Gaz	Hey! Look at this!

Superman 'fanfare'. The Guardian appears suddenly. Gaz and Dave leap back, very shocked.

Guardian	Stop, you two!
Gaz and Dave	Who are you?
Guardian	I'm the *(name of school/community)* Guardian. I'm sworn to stop all vandalism. My aim is to make thoughtless people like you a little kinder.
Gaz and Dave	What?!
Guardian	Would you like that on your house? *(Points to scrawl on the wall.)*
Gaz	My Dad would go mad.
Dave	I'd get anyone who wrote on our house.
Guardian	Well, you've made a mess of this school.

Dave *(Caretaker's name)* will get it off.

Guardian *(Caretaker's name)* isn't going to do your work for you.

Gaz and Dave Our work?!

Guardian *(In a loud, commanding voice)* You've made the mess and you're going to clean it up . . . and watch out: in future, I may be watching!

Gaz and Dave *(Now quaking with fear)* Y-y-yes, Guardian.

Guardian *(To audience)* Always try to think about other people, and be kind and considerate like the *(name of school/ community)* Guardian. *(Guardian thumps chest dramatically.)*

31. If we were all a little more considerate, the world would be a happier place. Let's sing this song together.

SONG

Choose one of these songs for the whole school to sing:
the theme from *Neighbours*, 'Stand Up, Clap Hands, Shout "Thank you, Lord"', or 'Think, think on these Things', or 'If I had a Hammer', all from *Someone's Singing, Lord*, published by A. & C. Black.

BACKDROP

To show the children the difference between our harvest and that of the Third World, display a simple bowl of rice on a white cloth on a separate plinth.

CHECKLIST

- Backdrop

- Children's seating arrangements

- Record-player

- Records: 'Autumn' from *The Four Seasons* by Vivaldi; 'Autumn Leaves', sung by Frank Sinatra

- Large clock face

- Warm clothes for one child

- Raincoat and wellies

- Picture or collection of fruits and nuts in a basket

- Bunches/paintings of chrysanthemums, dahlias, Michaelmas daisies

- Collection of hips, haws, blackberries

- Pine cones – one open, one closed (overnight soaking will ensure closure); and painting of these cones

- Painting/picture of a deciduous tree (bare or with leaves falling)

- Painting/picture of evergreen tree

- Leaf patterns and prints

- Seed patterns

- Poster/painting of toadstools

- Silhouette picture of migrating swallows

- Painting of squirrel

- Bulbs ready for planting, or picture

- Painting of fish or fishing boats

- Lump of coal and miner's helmet or painting of coal-mine

- Painting/poster of oil and gas platform or oil well

- A sukkah

- African masks, shakers and drums

- Play: *The Moon Cakes*
  costumes: peasant clothes for both sexes; cardboard breastplates, helmets, shields and swords for soldiers

- Poster/picture of Rama and Sita

- Row of candles

- Children's paintings of candles

- Bowl of sweets

- Small bowl of rice

- Hallowe'en costumes and masks

- Pumpkin/turnip masks/lanterns

- Guy in a wheelbarrow

- Warning posters about bonfire night

TOPIC WEB ▶

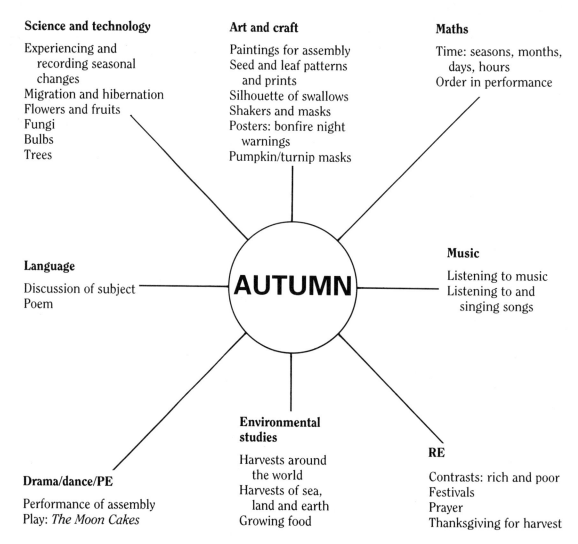

Science and technology

Experiencing and
  recording seasonal
  changes
Migration and hibernation
Flowers and fruits
Fungi
Bulbs
Trees

Art and craft

Paintings for assembly
Seed and leaf patterns
  and prints
Silhouette of swallows
Shakers and masks
Posters: bonfire night
  warnings
Pumpkin/turnip masks

Maths

Time: seasons, months,
  days, hours
Order in performance

Language

Discussion of subject
Poem

AUTUMN

Music

Listening to music
Listening to and
  singing songs

Drama/dance/PE

Performance of assembly
Play: *The Moon Cakes*

**Environmental
studies**

Harvests around
  the world
Harvests of sea,
  land and earth
Growing food

RE

Contrasts: rich and poor
Festivals
Prayer
Thanksgiving for harvest

MUSIC

For entry into the assembly play 'Autumn' from *The Four Seasons* by Vivaldi, or 'Autumn Leaves', sung by Frank Sinatra.

1. Good morning everyone.
   Welcome to our autumn assembly.
   Please sing this song with us.

SONG

Everyone sings 'Look for Signs that Summer's Done', from *Someone's Singing, Lord*, published by A. & C. Black.

2. Autumn is a beautiful season and lasts during
   the months of September, October and November.
   We can look out for lots of changes.

3. In autumn, the days grow shorter.
   We have to put our clocks back one hour.

   Child holds a large teaching clock, and puts the time back one hour.

4. We wear warmer clothes like jumpers and cardigans
   because the days become cooler.

   Child wears jumper/cardigan, or both.

5. I wear my raincoat and wellingtons to go out for walks
   on damp autumn days.

   Child wears these clothes.

6. We can look for fruits on trees, such as conkers, acorns,
   sycamore keys, beech nuts, apples, pears and plums.

   Child holds up painting.

7. The beautiful autumn flowers include chrysanthemums, dahlias and Michaelmas daisies.

Child holds up bunches of these flowers, or a painting of them.

8. In the hedges we can look for wild fruits such as blackberries, hips and haws.

Child holds up a plastic tray showing these fruits, collected on an earlier nature walk.

9. We can look for pine cones. When a pine cone is open, the weather will probably be fine.
When it is closed, it will probably rain.

Child holds up a painting. His or her neighbour holds up two cones, one open and the other closed (overnight soaking will ensure closure).

10. The leaves on the trees begin to change colour to red, yellow and golden brown, and they start to fall off.

POEM

This poem can be said by one child, two children or the whole class.

Falling Leaves

Twisting twirling, drifting down,
    Autumn leaves fall to the ground.
Floating, flying through the air,
    Autumn leaves are everywhere.

See them changing colours now,
    Red and yellow, gold and brown,
Leaves are blowing far and near
    Now that autumn-time is here.

11. Some trees keep their leaves.
These are called evergreen trees.

12. The trees that lose their leaves are called deciduous.

Children hold up pictures.

deciduous   evergreen

13. We made some patterns and prints with leaves.

Children hold up leaf patterns, prints and rubbings.

14. There are lots of seeds to be found and we made some patterns using seeds.

Children hold up some of their seed patterns.

15. On wet or damp mornings we sometimes see toadstools peeping through piles of leaves. Some of these are poisonous, so it is best not to touch any at all.

Child holds up picture or poster of different toadstools.

16. Other signs of autumn are the swifts and swallows getting ready to fly to warmer countries for the winter. This is called migration. We sometimes see the birds all lined up on telegraph wires. They wait until there is a big flock of them.

Child holds up silhouette picture.

17. Squirrels are looking for nuts to store away ready for the winter.

Child holds up a picture.

18. In our gardens and in the park the summer flowers are dying and it's time to plant bulbs for the spring.

Child holds up some bulbs or a picture of bulbs in the earth.

19. Harvest time comes in autumn and we have a harvest festival in church or school. Please sing this song with us.

SONG

The whole school can sing 'The Farmer comes to scatter the Seed', from *Someone's Singing, Lord*, published by A. & C. Black.

20. A harvest festival is to thank God for good crops of wheat, oats and barley, and for the fruit and vegetables that make up the harvest of the land.

Child points to relevant items on backdrop.

21. We thank God for all the fishes and creatures that make up the harvest of the sea.

Child holds up picture.

22. We thank God for the harvest of the earth, the coal, oil and gas that give us energy, heat and light.

Children could hold up lumps of coal, miner's helmet, a painting of an oil well and derrick and a painting/poster of a gas and oil platform.

SONG

At this stage the class could sing 'Paint Box' from *Harlequin*, published by
A. & C. Black.

23. There are lots of festivals in autumn.
Jewish people celebrate Sukkot.
This is also a harvest festival and it lasts eight days.

24. Jewish people sometimes build a small hut of branches
and leaves, called a tabernacle or sukkah,
and they eat beneath its shade.

One of these tabernacles could be built and included
in the harvest display.

Drape crepe paper across the top, to form a canopy.

paper leaves and
fruit hang from
the canopy

frame of rolled
newspapers covered
with green crepe

25. In some parts of West Africa the yam harvest
is celebrated. Yams are a kind of sweet potato.

26. The people take yams to their priest so that they can be
offered up to the gods.

27. During the festival plays are performed,
and there is plenty to eat and drink.

If there is a local African-origin community, you could get in touch to enlist their
help or parental help with a West African dance, which could be performed at this
point. The children could make masks, and musical instruments such as rattles and
drums from yoghurt cartons or tins which have been painted and decorated.

28. The people of China celebrate the Moon Festival
    in autumn. It takes place when the moon is full,
    and they make special moon cakes
    which they give to friends.

29. The children are allowed to stay up late,
    and they go out with their parents to watch
    the moon rise in the sky.

PLAY

The Moon Cakes

Characters
Two groups of children: peasants and soldiers;   five narrators.

Costumes
Peasant clothes for both sexes; cardboard breastplates, shields, helmets and swords
for the soldiers.

The action takes place on a bare stage; the story is told by the narrators and mimed
by the actors.

Narrator 1   Long ago a fierce tribe of people
            called the Mongols had become
            masters of China.

*Group of soldiers mime ordering group of peasants from one side of the stage
to the other.*

Narrator 2   The people were very frightened,
            too frightened even to talk
            to each other.

The peasants sit sadly while the soldiers stand guard over them.

Narrator 3   The Chinese made plans to win back
            their own land.
            They wrote secret messages to each other
            and baked them inside little cakes.

Peasants mime writing messages, mixing and baking cakes.

Narrator 4 They passed these cakes to each other
at night, so they called them moon cakes.

Peasants pass cakes to each other and then assemble into an army to fight the Mongols. They mime a fight and chase off the Mongol army.

Narrator 5 The moon cakes had helped to free the
people of China. Every year since,
they have held a festival to
help them remember.

30. Diwali is the most famous Hindu festival and it
takes place in autumn. It is a New Year festival,
a festival of light and a harvest festival, all in one.

31. It is a time when everyone wears new clothes,
cleans their houses and takes gifts of sweets
to friends and relations.

Child holds bowl of sweets.

32. It also celebrates the return of Rama and Sita
to their kingdom after they had been forced
to stay away for fourteen years.

Child holds up poster or picture.

33. They were guided home by thousands of lights
lit by the people of their kingdom.

Children hold up their own pictures of candles, decorated with glitter and metallic foil paper. Also a row of candles could be set up at the front of the hall and lit by the teacher. If the curtains are drawn it will add to the atmosphere. The class could sing the song 'Diwali' from Tinderbox, published by A. & C. Black.

Depending on when the assembly is held, you may wish to include Hallowe'en and bonfire night.

34. In autumn we have Hallowe'en and sometimes we play
trick or treat.

Children wearing Hallowe'en costumes and masks recite the following rhyme.

Hallowe'en is coming, coming soon,
Witches and ghosts will be after you.
We'll come round crying, "trick or treat",
And hope for lots of cakes and sweets.

35. We also remember Guy Fawkes and we make a guy to burn on the bonfire.

Child wheels in a wheelbarrow containing a guy. The whole class sings.

Remember, remember the fifth of November,
Gunpowder, treason and plot.
I see no reason why gunpowder treason
Should ever be forgot.

36. We should be very careful on bonfire night and follow the firework code.

Children hold up safety posters or paintings of their own.

37. We should always keep fireworks in a closed tin box.

38. We should make sure our pets are kept safely indoors so that they will not be frightened by the fireworks.

PRACTER

PRAYER

This prayer is said by a child at the front of the stage, holding a small bowl of rice; or one child can point to backdrop and hold up a bowl of rice while another reads.

Dear Lord,
Thank you for the changing seasons,
for the beauty and colours of autumn
and for the rich harvest.
Help us to remember those countries
where the harvest is not so good,
where the people may be hungry or starving,
and where this bowl of rice is all the food they have.
Help us to share our riches so that everyone
may live a happy and useful life.

Amen

WINTER

BACKDROP

silver, black and white snowflakes

30 cm

white and blue crepe strips, 8 cm wide, stapled at the top

CHECKLIST

- Backdrop
- Children's seating arrangements
- Record-player
- Record: 'Winter' from *The Four Seasons* by Vivaldi
- Snowflake headbands for the whole class
- Card showing the names of the seasons: 'Winter' in blue, to stand out
- Six posters: 'Winter is . . .'
- Painting of a rainy day
- Painting of a snowy day

- Clock face showing 9 o'clock
- Clock face showing half past three
- Picture of the school in winter
- Winter clothes for a boy and a girl
- Card displaying the word 'hibernation'
- Painting of hibernating hedgehog or mouse
- One 'glum' (a sad face painted on a paper plate)
- One 'smiley' (a happy face painted on a paper plate)
- Painting of a person slipping on ice
- Painting of cars in fog

144

- Painting of cars stuck in snow

- Poster: 'Drive carefully, please'

- Play: *Lost in the Ice*
  props: ladder made from corrugated paper; 'pond' made from a hoop covered with tinfoil; two stage blocks
  costumes: winter clothes for three children; leotard, tights, tail and mask for the dog

- Children's own writing and paintings about favourite winter activities

- Painting of Nativity

- Painting of Father Christmas

- Scarf and a piece of coal

- School bell

- Small basket containing bamboo, oranges and fern

- Red envelope

- Chinese paper lanterns

- Poster/painting of Chinese dragon dance

TOPIC WEB ▶

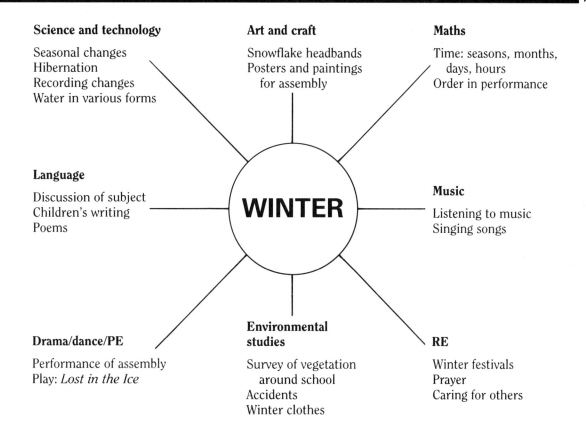

Science and technology

Seasonal changes
Hibernation
Recording changes
Water in various forms

Art and craft

Snowflake headbands
Posters and paintings
  for assembly

Maths

Time: seasons, months,
  days, hours
Order in performance

Language

Discussion of subject
Children's writing
Poems

WINTER

Music

Listening to music
Singing songs

Drama/dance/PE

Performance of assembly
Play: *Lost in the Ice*

Environmental studies

Survey of vegetation
  around school
Accidents
Winter clothes

RE

Winter festivals
Prayer
Caring for others

THE ASSEMBLY: Winter ▶

MUSIC

For entry into the assembly you could play 'Winter' from *The Four Seasons* by Vivaldi.

The class could all wear headbands with snowflakes of different colours attached to them.

Card headband

1. Good morning everyone.

2. On this cold day, our assembly is all about winter.

3. Winter is a time of year. It is one of the four seasons.

4. The seasons are spring, summer, autumn and winter.

Child holds up card with the names of the seasons written on it; 'Winter' in blue, to stand out.

5. We think winter is all of these things . . .

Child points to posters on display and says the words, or six children each hold up a poster and say the relevant word.

white paint on
black sugar paper

6. Winter is the coldest season.
   We usually get the worst weather in winter.

7. Here are a poem and some pictures about
   winter weather.

POEM

One child takes the part of 'snow' and another of 'rain'. They do appropriate actions: 'snow' wiggles fingers slowly as arms move gently from side to side from the head downwards; 'rain' pats two fingers loudly on the palm of the other hand. Two other children each hold up a painting – a rainy day and a snowy day.

8. Softly, softly falling so,
   This is how the snowflakes go.

9. Pitter-patter, pitter-patter,
   Pit pit pat.
   Down go the raindrops on my hat.

10. Can you guess what this is?

11. A white bird floats down through the air,
    And never a tree, but he lights there.

10. It's snow.

12. Snow is rain which freezes as it falls to earth.

13. Frost is the water droplets which are on everything.
    They freeze like little ice-lollies when it gets cold.

14. Winter can be very beautiful. Listen to this poem.

POEM

This poem can be read by the teacher or by an older child, possibly with a good reader from the class saying the first and last verse.

Jack Frost

Jack Frost he is a chilly fellow,
    Fingers long and white.
He touches wall and pane and hollow
    On a winter's night.

His breath is sparkling, hair is crystal,
    Glinting in the moon.
Best get in beside the fire,
    He'll come to your house soon.

His eyes are sapphires, icy-blue.
    He drapes the branches long
With tassles made of diamonds bright
    And sings a winter's song.

He covers fields o'er with his fingers,
Makes the world so bright.
Our breath is misty while he lingers;
Jack Frost's out tonight!

15. Can you guess what sort of weather this is about?

16. A house-full, a hole-full,
And you cannot gather a bowl-full.

15. It's fog. Fog is a bit like rain that is standing still,
but the drops are very tiny.

17. The drops of water are so close together
that we can't see through them.

18. Here is a song about thunder. Winter thunderstorms
are especially cold and horrid.

SONG

The whole class stands and sings this to the tune of 'Frère Jacques'.

Thunder

I hear thunder, I hear thunder,
Hark don't you, hark don't you?
Pitter-patter rain drops,
Pitter-patter rain drops,
I'm wet through, so are you.

19. The nights are longer in winter and the days
are shorter.

20. When we come to school at 9 o'clock
it is just getting light.

Child holds up a large clock face showing 9 o'clock.

21. When we go home at half past three
it is getting dark again.

Child holds up a large clock face showing 3.30.

22. When it is cold and dark in winter,
not many things grow. We looked round our school
and this is what we found.

Child points to large picture of the school, showing things that the class observed
during a pre-assembly survey. Speaker 23 points to and names specific items (amend
the following list as necessary).

23. Bare branches, mud, water, dead leaves, wet grass,
frost on the roof, . . .

24. We saw lots of children wearing warm winter clothes,
like these.

Speaker 24 and another child of the opposite sex wear outdoor winter clothes.

25. Lots of animals go to sleep in winter because it is cold
and there is not much food for them.
This is called hibernation.

Child holds up card showing the word 'hibernation'.

26. Hedgehogs, toads and dormice hibernate
in our country. They make a warm bed
and stay there all winter.

Child holds up picture of hibernating animal.

27. Animals grow warmer coats in winter.

28. In summer we cut off the sheep's winter coat and
make woolly jumpers from it, for us to wear in winter!

Child points to his or her own woollen jumper.

29. Winter can be cold and lonely for old people living
on their own.

30. They can't run around to keep warm like us.
    They could fall on icy slides, so don't make slides
    on pavements.

31. People are lonely when they haven't got any friends
    or family and would like some.

    Child holds up a 'glum' (a sad face drawn on a paper plate or card disc).

32. If you know any old people who live near you,
    ask Mum or Dad to take you to see them.

33. A visit may cheer someone up.

    Child holds up a 'smiley' (a happy face drawn on a paper plate or card disc).

34. Winter can be dangerous. Here's what can happen
    if you walk on an icy patch.

    Child holds up picture of someone slipping on ice.

35. Cars may skid on icy roads and crash in fog,
    when the drivers can't see.

    Child holds up picture of cars in the fog.

36. Cars get stuck in snow, too.

    Child holds up picture of snowbound cars.

37. Tell your mums and dads to drive very carefully
    in winter.

    Child holds up poster: 'Drive carefully, please'.

38. Here's a short play about *(name of character from
    your reading scheme, or made-up name)*.

PLAY

Lost in the Ice

Backdrop
Use assembly backdrop.

Props
Ladder made of corrugated card; pond made from a hoop covered in tinfoil; two stage blocks.

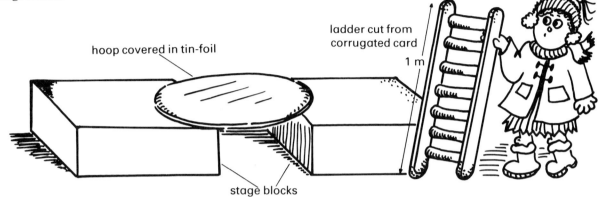

Characters
Boy, girl, adult, dog. (For these, you could use the names of characters in your reading scheme or current class reader.) Narrator.

Costumes
Outdoor winter clothes for the three human characters. A leotard, tights, tail and mask for the dog.

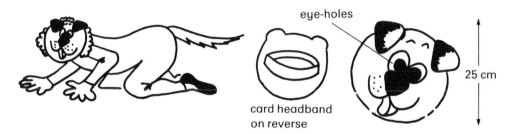

Narrator It was a cold winter's day. *(Boy's name)* and *(girl's name)* and *(dog's name)* went for a walk. They found that the pond had frozen over.

Boy, girl and dog enter and walk over to the 'pond'.

Boy Look, the pond has frozen over. I'm going to skate on it.

Girl Be careful. The ice might be too thin . . . oh, no!

Boy falls in the pond, i.e. steps into hoop and breaks tin-foil.

Boy   Oh help, help!

Girl   I can't reach you . . .
Quick *(dog's name)*, go and fetch someone.
(Boy's name) has fallen in the pond.

Dog   Woof, woof. *(Exits quickly.)*

Boy   Help, help!

Narrator   Off went *(dog's name)* as fast as he could.
He found *(adult's name)* and brought
him/her back.

Dog enters with adult, who is carrying the ladder.

Adult   Oh dear!
Hang on, I'll soon have you out of there.

Adult puts the ladder across the ground and pretends to crawl out towards the boy.

Adult   Grab hold of my hand. *(Stretches out hand.)*

Narrator   *(Adult's name)* helped the silly boy
to safety.
(Girl's name) was much more sensible.
She knew it wasn't safe to play
near frozen ponds or near any water.

Boy clambers out of the pond, helped by adult. All the actors come to the front and bow.

39. But winter can be great fun. Here are some of the things we like about winter.

Prior to the assembly, invite the class to write about and paint what they like about winter. Choose six of the children to read out what they have written and hold up their paintings. Topics could include skiing, slides, tobogganing, building snowmen, getting warm by the fire, bedtime.

40. There are lots of celebrations in winter.

41. Many people celebrate Christmas, when we remember
    Jesus' birthday and give each other presents.

    Child holds up painting.

42. We have Christmas trees and decorations and
    Father Christmas comes to our houses with presents.

    Child holds up painting or a pretend present.

43. There are many festivals in winter, all around
    the world.

44. Most of them celebrate the New Year.

45. In Scotland there is Hogmanay.
    There is a big party on New Year's eve.

46. There is also the ceremony of First Footing.
    This is when the very first visitor comes to the house
    after midnight, when the New Year begins.

47. The visitor must be a tall, dark man and he must
    bring coal for luck.

    Child is dressed in winter clothes with a scarf and carrying a piece of coal.

48. In England the churches ring out the old year with
    quiet bells, and ring in the new year with
    loud, happy bells.

    Child rings the school bell.

49. In Japan there is a festival which lasts for six days.

50. The people clean their houses extra well and
    decorate them with pine trees for long life, bamboo
    for honesty and ferns and oranges for good luck.

    Child holds a basket containing bamboo, oranges and a fern.

51. Jewish people celebrate the festival of Hanukkah. They light eight candles on a special candlestick, have parties and give presents.

Child holds candlestick or cut-out version.

52. The Chinese have a New Year festival too. They write good luck messages on lucky red paper and pin them round their doors.

53. The children get presents of money in lucky red envelopes.

Child holds red envelope, smiling.

54. Everybody visits their family and friends, and then they have a big celebration called the feast of the lanterns.

The children could make lanterns and show them at this point.

55. Each Chinese community has a big procession and the people make a huge dragon that dances through the streets.

Child holds up a poster or painting of the dragon dance. If your school has any connections with a Chinese community, you may be able to obtain first-hand information. You may even be able to arrange a dragon dance in school, as an extension of the assembly.

56. Muslim people have a quiet festival in the winter.

57. It is called Eid-ul-fitr. They have quiet prayers and thanksgiving and the children get presents.

58. So even though winter can be cold, lonely and dangerous it can also be a time for celebration and thanks.

59. Winter is many things. Let us pray.

PRAYER

This can be said by the whole class, or by one child while the others stand with hands together, eyes closed.

We thank you God for the beautiful changes in the seasons. Help us to enjoy winter and guard us from its dangers.

                    Amen

SONG

To end the assembly the class could sing one of these songs:

'See how the Snowflakes are Falling' or 'To God who makes all Lovely Things', both from *Someone's Singing, Lord*, published by A. & C. Black; 'January' or 'Ho, Jack Frost', both from *Harlequin*, published by A. & C. Black; 'In the Bleak Mid-winter', which can be found in most hymn books or carol collections; 'Winter' from *Every Colour Under the Sun*, published by Ward Lock Educational.

60. That is the end of our assembly about winter, and we hope we have given you something to think about.